What People Are Saying About
Daniel Edds and *Leveraging the Genetics of Leadership*

"Daniel Edds has the unique ability to explain what outstanding leaders create without delving into who they are. The inspired results he describes across a wide range of institutions attest to the abilities great leaders have to develop leaderful organizations. By distilling the essence of effective leadership *systems*, he shows us how to continuously tap the potential of each individual in service of a powerful whole. His systemic focus enables organizations to sustain high performance without depending on the capabilities of any one leader."

— David Peter Stroh, Social Systems Consultant and Best-Selling Author of *Systems Thinking for Social Change*

"Daniel Edds hits the ball out of the park with *Leveraging the Genetics of Leadership*. In it, he reveals too much has been written about personal leadership and not enough about how leadership needs to be thought of as a system we can implement in our workplaces so that when that dynamic leader leaves the company, the system continues to operate and the company to succeed. Brilliant!"

— Patrick Snow, Publishing Coach and International Best-Selling Author of *Creating Your Own Destiny* and *Boy Entrepreneur*

"Through a series of excellent examples based on personal interviews and meticulous research, Daniel Edds shows how individuals can turn around organizations by showing those organizations how to value a type of leadership that is systemic and inclusive so that everyone benefits, from the CEO to the employees at all levels to the customers. *Leveraging the Genetics of Leadership* is highly readable and highly invaluable."

— Tyler R. Tichelaar, PhD and Award-Winning Author of *When Teddy Came to Town*

"The vast majority of books on leadership fall into the trap of obsessing about the characteristics of the perfect leader. This is illusory because leaders always lead in relationship with followers, who themselves may also be leaders within their own contexts. An organization becomes effective because it works as a system—a set of functional parts interacting to achieve a purpose, and leadership is one such necessary part. Indeed, what if leadership itself is a system—a subsystem of the wider organization. If leadership is a system, engaged in relationships with other systems to create a high-performing, purposeful whole, it means that anybody with integrity and a reasonable level of emotional intelligence can learn how to lead. This is Daniel Edds' insight, gained from a consultancy career and deep conversations with the leaders of exceptional organizations. While 'systemic leadership' is a new buzzword in business and management schools around the world, Daniel comes straight from the sharp end of practice and delivers one of the most clearly written books I have seen in a while—with systemic insight, but unencumbered by jargon. Read and enjoy!"

— Gerald Midgley, Professor of Systems Thinking, Centre for Systems Studies, Business School, University of Hull, UK and 2013-2014 President of the International Society for the Systems Sciences

"Daniel Edds' *Leveraging the Genetics of Leadership* is full of truths about leadership that are often overlooked. Using a DNA metaphor, he reveals what creates a working system of leadership in an organization and how those elements can be used by the reader to replicate such a system in their own organization. This book will have you re-thinking everything you thought you knew about leadership and re-assembling it into a new model that truly works."

— Nicole Gabriel, Author of *Finding Your Inner Truth*
and *Stepping Into Your Own Becoming*

"In the sea of books on leadership, only a few are beginning to examine leadership as a system. A system of leadership, open to design, test, evaluation, and evolution—adaptive to change and tuned for the twenty-first century. Dan Edds is among those few looking for systemic change. In *Leveraging the Genetics of Leadership*, he provides fresh insights based on case studies and personal interviews. His systems approach to leadership is replicable and scalable from the smallest to the most complex organizations."

— Richard Hodge, PhD and Author of A Systems Approach to Strategy and Execution in National Security Enterprises and Faculty Member at Thought Leaders Business School, Australia

"Dan Edds gets it right! Our world needs an updated kind of leadership: an adaptive leadership system tailored to the DNA—the purpose, the culture, and the resources—of that specific organization."

— Cory Bouck, Author of The *Lens of Leadership: Being the Leader* Others WANT to Follow

"*Leveraging the Genetics of Leadership* is revolutionary. It shifts our paradigm from looking at leadership as a discrete personal choice to leadership as a system that can be understood and designed to give the desired output for any organization. This book articulates how organizations can harness leadership, consistently and continuously, by looking at it as a system."

— Elekanyani Ndlovu, Energy Sector Senior Executive, Professional Electrical Engineer (Pr. Eng), Non-Executive Director, Entrepreneur, Systems and Design Thinker, Johannesburg, South Africa

"After thirty-one years of law enforcement service, I have led during times of major crisis including violence, riots, cyclical drug epidemics, and a high school mass shooting. I have seen the destruction and turmoil associated with human frailty and predatory criminal behavior. Dan Edds' book *Leveraging the Genetics of Leadership* is written for such a time as this when police leaders and public servants need to apply a systems approach to institutionalize effective leadership values strategically so that police officers do the right thing for the right reason at the right time. The ideas and methodology of the book provide a clear roadmap and understanding that will, no doubt, enhance community-police relations. It is a 'must read' for all law enforcement leaders!"

— Rick Smith, Doctorate of Business
Administration and Chief of Police (Ret.)

"Daniel Edds has performed a great labor for all students of leadership. He has identified the vital few principles and practices from the trivial many. If leadership is a system, if it's greater than the sum of its parts, what is that system? What are the component parts? How do those mutually reinforcing parts work together? And finally, how can leaders perpetuate a leadership system to live after them? This book is a gift for any leader who has been given the stewardship to lead, but doesn't know how to approach it. A wonderful contribution to the leadership literature!"

— Timothy R. Clark, PhD, Author of *The 4 Stages of Psychological Safety: Defining the Path to Inclusion and Innovation*

"Dan Edds' *Leveraging the Genetics of Leadership* makes an important contribution to understanding effective leadership by introducing the concept of developing a leadership system versus developing "superhero" leaders. More than twenty years ago, I was first exposed to a leadership system as we applied the leadership methods used by the Toyota Corporation to healthcare at Virginia Mason Medical Center.

If I'd had Dan's insights at that time, together with his stories of leaders who are creating leadership systems in their own organizations, it would have made the journey a little easier. I have experienced the power of what Dan describes as a leadership system—focusing your efforts as a leader on developing and creating value versus managing/controlling, tapping into every person's wisdom and knowledge, and using failure to learn. Dan's book ultimately serves as an inspiration combined with offering practical advice for leaders who want to create a high-performing organization."

— Sarah Patterson, Executive Director, Virginia Mason Institute, Seattle, Washington

A TRANSFORMATIONAL ROADMAP FOR ENGAGING YOUR WORKFORCE

LEVERAGING THE GENETICS OF LEADERSHIP

CRACKING THE CODE OF SUSTAINABLE TEAM PERFORMANCE

DANIEL B. EDDS, MBA

AVIVA
PUBLISHING
New York

ACKNOWLEDGMENTS

I cannot imagine anyone writing a book without massive support from many people. The same is true for me. Tell people you are researching and writing about leadership and everyone has a story. Surprisingly, most were great stories. One or two even made it into the book. Here is an all-too-brief list of those whose contributions were absolutely vital.

Scott Ausenhuse. Scott holds a PhD in Biochemistry and a JD. He spends his days as a patient attorney in the biopharmaceutical industry. With his two PhDs, I felt I had found a good source to explain DNA as a possible metaphor for an organizational system. Over dinner, I asked him to give me the middle school lesson on genetics. By the time we were finished, I was asking for the kindergarten lesson. Nevertheless, I came away thinking it an amazing system that beautifully explains the raw power of systems thinking and the opportunity it creates for organizational leadership.

General Barry McCaffrey (Retired). General McCaffrey had been on my interview radar for two years before I reached out to him. Now a year after my interview, I am still reeling. Our one-hour conversation was the most profound, mind-bending hour of my career. If there is anything about organization leadership he does not know, it is not worth knowing.

Barbara Kellerman, PhD. Dr. Kellerman is one of the few, but growing number of thought leaders and researchers who are challenging the current multibillion-dollar leadership development industry—an industry that she says has not only failed to produce better leaders, but given us worse leaders. She even takes on her own institution, Harvard University. When I first reached out to her in the very early days of my research, I was honored when she wrote right back with encouragement and thoughtful critique. When we spoke on the phone about how one of the nation's most successful hospitals intentionally develops people, she knew exactly what I was seeing and directed me to additional research material, which became the foundation for this book's second section.

Eric Moll and the Entire Team at Mason General Hospital and Its Family of Clinics. Eric and his team gave me the high privilege of leading them through designing their leadership system when the idea was still in the embryonic stage of development.

Jennie Nash. Jennie is an extraordinary book coach who was kind enough to tell me my case studies were powerful, "but the rest of it is pretty boring." While she did everything an author could want in a book coach, Jennie did something far more important: She gave my voice permission to speak. In working with Jennie, I was never sure if I was working with a book coach or a therapist.

Roger Nelson, Ed.S, Roger was more than gracious in reading every word of an early manuscript and pronouncing it to be the solution to all things wrong with public education. While his exuberance was a bit generous, the compliment was enough to know I was onto something special.

Toby Rawlinson. Toby is a random guy I met on an airplane one day who opened his world of friends to me and whose contributions confirmed the validity of this new approach to leadership.

Greg Roberts, MSW. After one of my first public presentations Greg gave me the high honor of a compliment and offer to read the manuscript in draft. He read every word and in addition to several improvements to the content gave me an edit worthy of a professional editor.

Tom Snyder. Tom is an RN, BSN, MBA, CLSSBB, FACHE, and Regional Director of Oregon Region Quality Management and Medical Staff Services Operations, Providence Health & Services—Oregon Region. Tom was kind enough to read every word of my first draft and honest enough to tell me to put a little more of my right brain into the manuscript—that would be the more artistic and creative side.

Kyle Usrey, JD. Kyle is the Vice President of Academic Affairs at Colorado Christian University. Kyle is a brilliant scholar with a generous heart to help those who ask for his help. He gave me an entire day and with his keen mind helped me to think critically about the model of a leadership system. On the plane back home, I reworked the basic model, and it has not changed since then.

Theo Yu. Unexpectedly, Theo and I found ourselves on parallel journeys. While he was conducting research for his PhD thesis in transformational leadership, he, like me, began discovering evidence of systems at work. My discoveries were in hospitals and manufacturing organizations. His discoveries came from working with a hurricane-stricken community in the Philippines and regularly serving Sunday evening meals to the homeless in his hometown.

My son Jason. I thank him for his encouragement and willingness to listen to his dad and then give me a millennial's perspective.

My wife Kaye. For three years, she has been the foundation in this journey, and for thirty-one years, the one whose encouragement means more to me than I can express.

CONTENTS

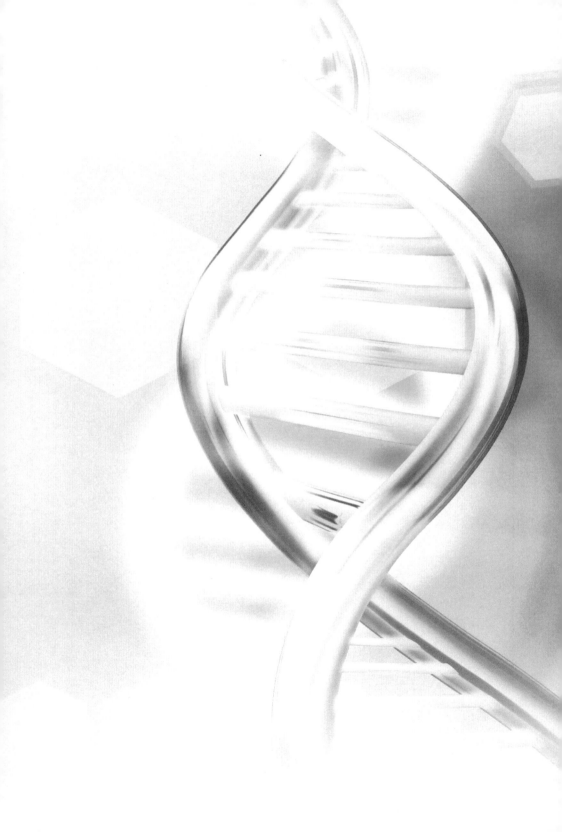

PREFACE

"Be willing to be a beginner every single morning."

— Meister Eckhart

I had spent four days conducting a Lean *"kaizen"* event for a large state agency. We had analyzed core business processes. We had value stream maps displayed on a large wall. We had a spaghetti diagram of the agency's office that showed that every invoice had to pass the financial manager's desk up to seven times before it was ever paid. We had designed four process improvement initiatives that would have eliminated redundant work, focused the organization on high value work, improved customer service, and allowed the team greater pride in their organization. At times, the work was intense. Other times, it was pure euphoria as the team saw displayed on a wall the amazing work they did and how each of them had to do the miraculous every month to complete their mission. At the end of the four days, one of the most experienced leaders physically grabbed the manager by the lapels of his sport coat, lifted him off his feet, shook him, and said, "If you don't do something with this, don't ever ask me to participate in something like this ever, ever again." Out of courtesy, we briefed the department's executive leadership on the project's outcome. The executives were pleased. The State had a new governor who had campaigned on a platform of a more efficient government. He had even announced that Lean would be his methodology to lower the cost of government. These executives could proudly report that they were implementing the governor's mandate. Except, that is where all the work stopped. Not one initiative was ever implemented. The investment of four days, with eighteen professionals, who were already overloaded and had sacrificed to be involved, was flushed down the toilet.

As much as I would love to say the failure with this State client was an outlier, an anomaly, the reality is that it was more the norm than the exception. During more than twenty-five years as a management consultant, I have seen this same phenomenon more times than I care to admit. However, this event crystalized for me that something else was going on. The department's senior leadership were smart, well-educated, and by any measure, highly qualified to do their jobs. They were not bad managers, but they were working in a system that rewarded them for their proximity to the governor. The system did not require them to consider the input of lower ranking staff, to work to continuously improve processes that would create more value for their stakeholders, or to eliminate work that had no value so their staff could go home on time. It was easier to pay overtime.

Two years later, the CEO of a rural county hospital asked me to help him design a formal model of leadership. I told him that, in my opinion, leadership was more about the system than a group of individuals; therefore, our first task would be to identify the system's output. He said, "That's exactly what I want to do." Nine months later, I walked away from that project believing it was the single most important project of my career and the solution to the problems I was seeing in virtually every organization I have worked with.

The realization that leadership can be a designed system catapulted me into a journey that has become nearly obsessive. I had to start from the foundation. What exactly is a system, and what does a system of leadership look like? I would eventually turn to Donella Meadows, one of the giants in systems theory. Her definition of a system informed my understanding of leadership as an organizational system. Once I knew what to look for, I began to see systems of leadership in some rather unusual places, including such diverse groups as the New York Mafia, the Salvation Army, the US Army, a local elementary school, and an international industrial giant.

I also discovered that outside of a few academics, few people are talking about leadership as an organizational system. Those who do walk up to the line, but then they turn around to talk about personal leadership. However, one person who boldly proclaims that leadership is a system is Barbara Kellerman, PhD, of Harvard University's John F. Kennedy School of Government. She is running at the tip of the spear to challenge how we commonly think about leadership. Her encouragement, support, and mentoring have been invaluable in writing this book.

In the following pages, I won't be telling you anything about the elements of quality leadership that you have not already read dozens of times. But I will show you how to organize the elements differently. The stakes could not be higher. The common understanding of a leader as someone who acquires a following is not only archaic, but catastrophically failing to psychologically, intellectually, or emotionally engage the workforce. By some estimates, nearly 80 percent of the workforce is not happy with their work. In other words, the workforce is stuck working in organizations where mediocrity is fully accepted. At the same time, businesses and organizations of all types are crying for innovation. All the while, the greatest innovative force in the world walks in the door every morning. We have the most highly educated and creative workforce in the planet's history. From my experience, it is a workforce that will readily contribute, sacrifice, engage, and innovate if current leadership systems would just get out of its way.

I believe the next generation's opportunity will not be to acquire and implement more technology, but to design the ways humans must interact to unleash the basic human capacity for innovation, creativity, and transformation. If we can do this, the possibilities are endless.

Please join me on this journey to innovate leadership as an organizational system.

Daniel B. Edds, MBA

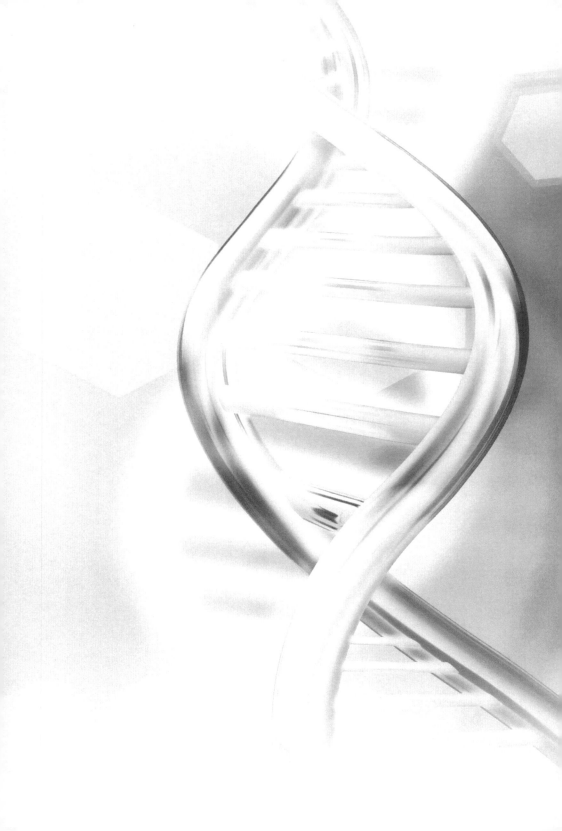

LEVERAGING THE POWER OF THE SYSTEM

"The fact is that the system that people work in...may account for 90 or 95 percent of performance."

— W. Edwards Deming

This is not your typical book on leadership. Most books on the subject fall within two broad categories. The first is the autobiography. These provide the writer with an opportunity to solidify their personal legacy. The second category of books on leadership describes personality traits of widely respected leaders. However, if we sum up all the leadership laws and personal traits considered essential to a good leader, no combination of Jesus, St. Francis of Assisi, Mahatma Gandhi, Martin Luther King, Jr., Winston Churchill, Franklin Delano Roosevelt, Abraham Lincoln, and Nelson Mandela will ever be able to model all of them. At my last count, Amazon had 197,000 such books. The world does not need another. If this is what you are looking for, sorry to disappoint.

However, another kind of leadership book exists—such books are fewer in number, but more valuable. They take a serious look at leadership from an organizational perspective and seek to provide solutions to make organizations places of creativity, innovation, and value creation for all stakeholders. My mission in writing this book is to demonstrate how highly successful organizations performing at elite levels are innovating the very foundations of leadership. They are abandoning the notion of the mythic leader, the *one* who will lead them to the promised land of corporate success. Instead, they are custom-designing a kind of organizational DNA or genetic code that is not dependent on inspirational personalities, charisma, or visionaries.

A never-ending conversation exists about the need for leaders who are bold, innovative, confident, and creative. Frankly, I no longer believe in this myth. In fact, I get angry every time I hear someone talk about bold and courageous leadership. The great need of our day is for a courageous workforce, which requires unleashing the creativity and ingenuity that every human has in abundance by the virtue of being human. The challenge today is creating organizational systems that unleash these basic capacities within the workforce rather than suffocate them. If leaders and emerging leaders stop fixating on personal courage and innovation and start designing systems, building a cultural genetic code for the workplace that unleashes these human capacities in their staff, we would launch a tidal wave of institutional creativity and innovation, while making the workplace somewhere humans thrive.

Therefore, what I offer is a leadership approach that focuses on leadership systems, a kind of organizational DNA, rather than traits of the individual leader. This approach will be comprehensive, new, bold, innovative, thoughtful, demanding, and for some, terrifying. I will demonstrate how it can be applied to your personal leadership, team leadership, and company. It is an understanding of organizational leadership that can be scaled to fit the local elementary school with seventy-five educational leaders or the US Army with 2 million active duty and reserve personnel and every organization in between. It is an approach that will generate a powerful employee experience, turn the workforce into your most vocal ambassadors, and make the company brand more than syrupy marketing slogans. It is an approach that will change us socially, economically, and personally. If this kind of leadership is what you want, then welcome. It is my pleasure to introduce you to the next generation of leadership innovation—a system of organizational design—a system that can be designed to a specific genetic code that will build an authentic employee experience, separating you from the competition. To explain how this works, I will start with a rather simple but personal story.

When my son Jason was in sixth grade, he tried out for the school basketball team. Actually, the idea of a tryout is a bit of a stretch. He attended a private school so small that they did well just to field a team. Basically, every boy who wanted to play got to play. The result was a team with no superstar athletes and modest expectations, at best. Will, their young coach, had played basketball in college, but he had little coaching experience. Still, he liked kids, was a part-time youth worker, and needed some extra money to further his schooling.

What Will lacked in experience, he more than made up for with the system he used, designed to produce unselfish team play. His practices, rules, and behavior requirements for himself and his young athletes were designed to promote the team. If one of the boys lost his temper or wanted to hog the ball, he was pulled until he cooled down, no matter the score. Will, himself, was a model of professional courtesy. In three years watching Will and his assistants coach, I never once saw any of them raise their voice in anger at anyone. I wish that had been the case with many of his competitors.

As much as I would love to say this young team placed first in their league, the disappointing reality is that these boys lost every game. As a dad, it was heartbreaking to watch my son and his friends play their hearts out only to lose every time. But despite the crushing losses, no one quit. I think something about learning to play for and with each other prevented anyone from quitting—they would have been quitting on their best friends, letting the entire team down.

The second year, the team did a little better. They won about half their games.

The third year, the unthinkable happened. They went undefeated. The same group of boys, from a small school that could barely put together a team, won every game that year against larger schools. I am not sure who was more excited, those boys or the parents, but I know Coach Will will always be one of my favorite people because he gave my son an experience I wish every child could have at least once while growing up.

While Coach Will taught his boys basic ball handling skills and shooting techniques, he also engineered a kind of DNA for how they would play the game together. It was not about winning or losing. It was playing the game to a specific code that empowered them to play well as a team. This code gave them the best opportunity to win. Within this system, every boy was empowered to do what he did best to contribute to the team. It was a system designed to take the natural competitiveness of young boys and channel that energy into the team. The result was each boy and the team overall enjoyed the thrill of being champions. Furthermore, Coach Will understood that his system did more than produce great team play; it also gave the team something of greater value. He did not see his team as just basketball players but as boys who would soon become young men, and he knew the lessons they learned from him could last a lifetime. And, yes, this dad still gets teary-eyed just thinking about it.

I am not at all suggesting that the system Coach Will designed could have produced an undefeated championship season without talent. John Wooden, legendary coach of the UCLA Bruins, had an extraordinary system for his basketball teams. On the way to winning seven consecutive national championships, he also enjoyed brilliant athletes. His system refined and focused their talent toward team play. While seldom talking about winning or losing, he put together a record that may never be broken.

This simple story of a small school basketball team demonstrates several lessons that can be transferred to organizational performance—but one is critical.

Systems always produce more than the sum of the individual parts. In short, systems take one plus one and create ten. Phosphate and sugar are the basic elements in a DNA molecule. They are simple elements found in virtually every household kitchen. Yet their design allows them to interact, and from that interaction springs the foundation of all biological life. Similarly, the right system will take young boys of modest athletic talent and turn them into champions.

In this book, we will look at how in the same way, Captain David Marquet, captain of the *USS Santa Fe*, designed a system of leadership that took the lowest-performing nuclear-powered attack submarine in the fleet and made it the highest-performing submarine in US Navy history in just two years—with virtually the same crew. We will also see how a Native American healthcare organization went from an embryo to receiving the nation's highest award for excellence by creating a system of care that celebrates Native American spiritual values while generating clinical outcomes that rank with the nation's best. This book will demonstrate how healthcare systems, manufacturing companies, a local elementary school, and even the US Army are custom-designing their leadership DNA into an organizational system. The result is a workforce engaged in driving innovation and generating unparalleled, sustainable performance.

Why This and Why Now?

I had just finished a project for a large state agency. It had gone well, and even though the resulting system would take eighteen months to implement, I saw hope at the end of the tunnel. In my last conversation with the deputy director, she confessed, "I don't tell my friends where I work; it would be too embarrassing." Over my twenty-five-year career in consulting, I have heard various versions of this dozens of times, but never so bluntly. Frankly, I find it disgusting that so many leaders accept mediocrity, and in doing so, lock their workforce into a culture where they will never be champions. It is outrageous when leaders knowingly and willingly subject their workforce to mediocrity.

No one should ever be ashamed of where they work. Despite all the rhetoric about people being our most important asset, for the most part, it is just lip service intended to inspire the workforce. The data shows the reality is very different. This book is largely my attempt to give voice to the millions of smart, hardworking people stuck in organizations where mediocracy rules. In its 2017 report, "State of the American Workplace," Gallup reports that more than 50 percent of the workforce is non-engaged—they go to work, do their job, collect a paycheck, and go home. They contribute little to innovation and creating customer value.

Gallup reports that another 16 percent are actively sabotaging the workplace. And six in ten millennials are actively looking for a new job at any given point. George Clifton, chairman of Gallup, concludes, "The American leadership philosophy simply doesn't work anymore." He goes on to say, "America needs to historically transform the practice of management similar to the way Six Sigma and Lean management improved processes in the 1980s."

In the same report, Gallup documents that in the highest-performing organizations, 70 percent of the workforce is engaged, driving innovation and customer value. These organizations have better productivity, higher customer satisfaction, provide greater value, and enjoy lower costs and higher profits. The research culminating in this book demonstrates that organizations that consistently perform at the highest levels approach leadership differently. Instead of focusing on developing individual leaders, they design and develop better leadership systems and then train and coach their leaders to the requirements of their system. Like Coach Will, who designed a system of playing basketball and then trained young boys how to play to the requirements of the system. The result is championship performance. Metaphorically, organizational leadership becomes a symphony as opposed to a group of soloists.

What You Are About to Discover

When I started this project, I had no real idea what I would find. It took months of research to discover what a leadership system looked like. However, as the structure began to unfold, every time I found evidence of a designed system, I found an organization or individual performing at elite levels. I also found something more. I met and discovered hospital executives, manufacturing CEOs, team leaders, and a school principal who were doing more than just building great organizations and teams. They were changing people's lives in ways that went way beyond their jobs. Just like Coach Will prepared young boys to become young men, these leaders were unleashing the workforce's creative energy in ways that capture economic and/or operational opportunity, while workers are allowed to grow and develop into better human beings.

In these pages, I will introduce you to some remarkable men and women and the organizations they lead. A few you may recognize. Most you will not. I doubt any of them will ever grace the cover of a national publication. They are too busy recreating the workplace to worry about a national reputation. But they are leaders who have stumbled upon a systemic approach to leadership. By following this intensely adaptable and flexible structure, you can join them in creating a new world of work. A world where people feel safe, where they sacrificially contribute, where they innovate every day, and where they create new customer value. As you read these pages, I hope you will see when we take personality out of leadership and replace it with structured organizational DNA that the opportunities for personal growth, organizational innovation, and sustainable performance becomes endless. Anyone can do what the people and organizations profiled in these pages are doing. No inspirational personality or brilliant futuristic vision is required.

So, if you are ready to discover a new world of leadership, leadership as a designed organizational system, let's get to it.

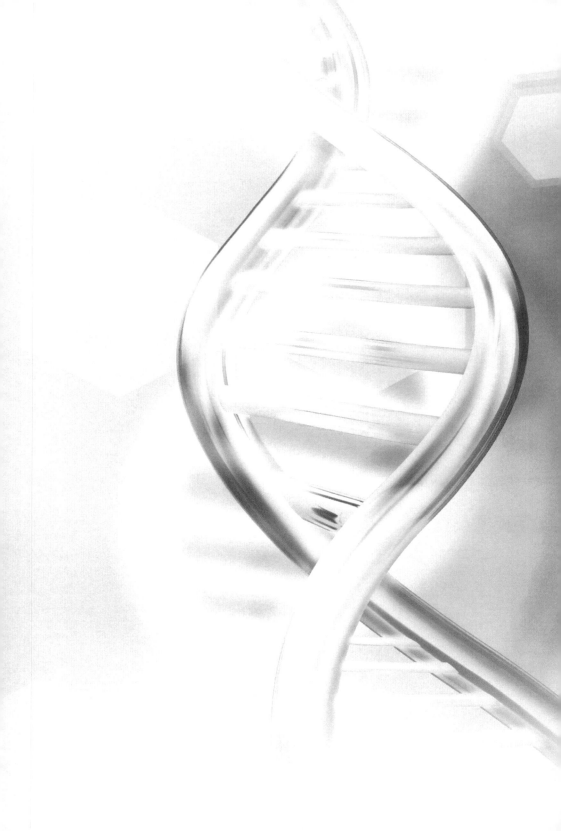

DESIGNING THE GENETIC CODE

I think of leadership now as a system—the "leadership system."
— Barbara Kellerman, PhD, Harvard Kennedy School

Deoxyribonucleic acid—DNA—is a molecule composed of two chains that coil around each other to form a double helix. This double helix carries a genetic code that dictates development, function, growth, and reproduction. Every time a cell in the human body splits, three billion digits of code must be replicated. This happens upwards of two trillion times a day. If a single strand of DNA were to be stretched out, it would be six feet long. If all the strands of DNA in your body were to be hooked together and stretched out, they would stretch between the earth and the sun, sixty-one times. That is a lot of DNA. This replication follows a precise process and is constantly monitored by the cell. In the rare event of an error, the cell sends in a repair team to mend the damage. This is a molecular system.

Fortunately for us, organizational DNA is not nearly so complex, yet the power that lies at the heart of a system is the same. A few common elements interact in a specific way to produce a single purpose or outcome. In the case of human DNA, the purpose or outcome is biological life. Forward-thinking individuals and organizations are beginning to realize they can custom-engineer their organizational DNA to a specific genetic code that will unleash the basic human capacities for creativity, innovation, and problem solving. The result is unparalleled

37

organizational performance. Consequently, we will be using DNA and organizational genetics as a metaphor for leadership as a designed organizational system.

The most common question I get when I mention leadership as a designed organizational system goes something like this, "Is this mechanized leadership or leadership by the numbers?" Here is my response:

- DNA's internal processes are extremely precise, yet it produces unimaginable diversity and complexity. Yet, opportunity still exists for adaption. I have a shrub in my backyard that normally has long and narrow leaves. Yet because I put it in a place of shade, it has adapted to the shade and now has long and wide leaves so it can capture more sunlight.

- Conventional wisdom says that manufacturing companies need to be in places where labor costs are low. Yet in the following pages, I will introduce you to a manufacturing company that flourishes in an area with some of the highest labor and housing costs in the nation. How? It trains its leaders precisely in how to be coaches and mentors to those they lead in the process of eradicating waste in their manufacturing processes. The result: Their customers receive so much value from the relationship that the company can pick and choose the customers it will serve.

- Systems can be redesigned and reengineered. When Captain David Marquet took command of the *USS Santa Fe*, a nuclear-powered attack submarine, the system of leadership he was trained in could not work. So, he redesigned a new system of leadership that could and did work.

When I read *Turn the Ship Around* by David Marquet, I found an extraordinarily clear system of leadership. It was a system Marquet designed from the ground up, or more appropriately, from the keel up. In this chapter, I will use Captain Marquet's story to illustrate the basic structure of a leadership system. The system he genetically engineered to channel the energy, intelligence, and passion of 135 sailors into one thing—making a submarine operate at maximum capacity.

***

December 1998, Pearl Harbor, Hawaii.

The USS Olympia, a nuclear-powered attack submarine, was heading out sea. It was one of the finest in the US Navy's fleet and designed to hunt down, stalk, and kill the enemy. Within a month, Captain David Marquet would assume command. He had spent a year learning every wire, bolt, valve, and system of this specific submarine. He knew the crew and their backgrounds. Technically, he was an expert on this particular submarine, and commanding it was his lifelong dream. He had spent his entire naval career preparing for this moment—taking command of a US Navy submarine. He would command based on a time-honored tradition. Because he was in charge, he would give orders and the sailors would execute them because he was the technical expert of this specific submarine.

Except, in a last-minute change, Marquet was given command of the USS Santa Fe, a Los Angeles-Class Nuclear Attack Submarine. Though newer, it was the laughingstock of the fleet. No one wanted to sail on it. Reenlistments were low, officer retention was zero, and training programs were rated "not effective." Furthermore, it was a different ship entirely. Its diving planes were located in the bow of the ship rather than in the sail (the tower-like structure that sits atop of the hull). Besides four torpedo tubes, it also had twelve vertical-launch Tomahawk land-attack missile tubes. It had a different reactor, different acoustics, and of course, a different crew. Marquet's ability to lead and give orders based on his superior technical brilliance evaporated the minute he walked on board. His crew knew more about the ship than he did.

On his first training cruise as captain, Marquet ran a standard drill to test the crew's ability to operate on battery power, simulating a reactor shutdown and restart. Batteries expend energy based on load, so to test his crew to see how they responded under pressure, he ordered the navigator, who had two years' experience on the ship, to speed up, "ahead two thirds." The navigator, in turn, ordered the helmsman "ahead two thirds." The helmsman should have turned a dial to read two thirds—but nothing happened.

On this ship, there was no two thirds on the electric motor. Captain Marquet had given a command that could not be carried out to a subordinate who knew it could not be carried out but who issued the command anyway to another subordinate who was incapable of carrying out the command. Since Marquet was not the technical expert on the ship, he had to rely on the technical expertise of each individual sailor.

Captain Marquet had to find another way to lead.

His leadership would require him to respect, incorporate, and develop the intelligence and training of his workforce—a workforce trained to operate some of the world's most complex technical, nuclear, and mechanical systems. These systems are fully integrated and stuffed inside a steel tube so 135 sailors can silently operate in the depths of the oceans and attack the enemy.

Marquet went about changing leadership's mathematical equation. In his book *Turn the Ship Around*, he explains, "Instead of one captain giving orders to 134 men (at the time submarine crews were all male), we would have 135 independent, energetic, emotionally committed, and engaged men thinking about what we needed to do and ways to do it right."[1] To create a new system of leadership that intentionally created a crew who was psychologically and intellectually engaged was more than simply tinkering with his personal leadership style. He was firing a torpedo with a high explosive warhead into the gut of an antiquated system of leadership.

WHAT IS A SYSTEM?

(This is the technical stuff.)

Donella Meadows is one of the giants in systems theory. Her book, *Thinking in Systems: A Primer*, is a classic and widely considered a must read. My definition of a leadership system simply builds on her general definition. Without getting too technical, here is my definition of a leadership system:

> A systematic model of leadership that comprehensively designs the way key organizational resources interact so that they achieve a desirable and measurable purpose or outcome.

This system has three parts: 1) key resources, 2) the specific interaction of those resources, and 3) the intentional purpose or outcome produced from those interactions. In keeping with the DNA metaphor, the outcome can be likened to the genetic backbone—the resources and the information of how they interconnect are the genes that make the system work. This DNA is like the source code of your operating system. Graphically, it looks like this:

---

1 Marquet, L. David. *Turn the Ship Around!* New York, NY: Penguin Publishing Group. Kindle Edition, 2012. Kindle location 1396.

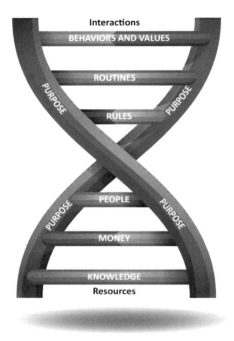

I will be using the system Marquet designed to illustrate the various parts of an organizational system of leadership. It is one of the clearest I have found, which most likely contributed to its success. I will not be describing the entire system Marquet designed, just the highlights.

DESIGNING THE DNA OF A SYSTEM'S OUTCOME OR PURPOSE

A system's purpose or outcome is the most powerful part of any system. Every other part of the system hangs on the outcome. Only a system has the internal power to intentionally scale the purpose across all segments of the workforce When Marquet writes, "We would have 135 independent, energetic, emotionally committed and engaged men thinking about what we needed to do and ways to do it right," every officer onboard the submarine knew the outcome the captain intended for both their organizational and personal leadership.

You will also notice the outcome of the system results in the intentional experience of the crew. I saw this in each organization I found operating consistently at elite levels. For Marquet and the sailors aboard the *USS Sante Fe*, turning around the ship meant turning around the crew's experience. The system's outcome was that the crew could expect to be emotionally committed and engaged. As Meadows says, "the least obvious part of the system, its function or purpose, is often the most crucial determinant of the system's behavior."[2]

System Pupose: Correlates with
the Employee Experience

DESIGNING THE DNA OF SYSTEM RESOURCES

Every organization operates with three key resources: people, money (in its broadest sense), and knowledge/information. One fundamental difference I found between high and mediocre performance is: high-performing organizations see these resources as opportunities to develop and create value, while mediocre organizations see them as assets to be managed (controlled).

Managing vs Developing
System Resources

2 Meadows, Donella H. *Thinking in Systems: A Primer*. Chelsea Green Publishing, 2008. Kindle Edition. Kindle Locations 445-446.

Developing the Resource of People. When Marquet decided he wanted a ship of 135 leaders rather than a ship with one leader and 134 followers, he had to take a very different approach to developing his crew. Because he needed a technically superior crew, he could not rely on their passive reading, study, and learning habits in preparation for their promotion exams. Furthermore, if he wanted them to be "engaged men thinking about what we needed to do and ways to do it right," they would also need the self-confidence to speak up and take intentional action when they saw an opportunity to improve the ship's performance. Just as Coach Will was not just developing basketball players, so Marquet's system had to develop both professional and personal capabilities of his crew.

Developing the Resource of Money. High-performing organizations look at money differently. Rather than seeing money as a set of inputs and outputs, they see it as a resource that can be developed to generate ever-increasing value. The more efficiently they use that resource, the more value they deliver to their customers.

In 2010, it took $150,000 to recruit and train one sailor. When Marquet saw that engaged sailors were much more likely to reenlist, he saw a double benefit: 1) increasing reenlistments would reduce recruitment and training costs, and 2) increasing reenlistments meant retaining very expensive intellectual capital, namely, sailors. By designing a system of leadership that developed and retained sailors, he could grow the value of human resources and make the submarine operate at ever higher levels.

Developing the Resource of Knowledge and Information. It's hard to imagine innovating the complex technical, scientific, and mechanical systems that make up a nuclear-powered submarine. Yet the crew of the *Santa Fe* found ways to solve problems, better ways of operating, and different ways of looking at operations. Discovery is the essence of innovation, and they did it by embracing a most unlikely resource—inspectors. Sailors operating a submarine feel the same way as administrators of hospitals, owners of restaurants, and managers of manufacturing plants: inspectors are viewed as intrusive and interfering. As Marquet began to deploy a leadership system that focused on developing the leader within each sailor, the sailors began looking for solutions to problems rather than waiting for an officer to tell them what to do. They found a rich source of intellectual and operational capital in an unlikely source—inspectors. They decided inspectors were not the enemy but an invaluable resource that could be used to improve their operation. The result was some of the highest operating scores in Navy history.

DESIGNING THE DNA OF SYSTEM INTERCONNECTIONS

When Captain Marquet determined that he needed a submarine of 135 sailors who were "Independent, energetic, emotionally committed and engaged men thinking about what we needed to do and ways to do it right," he had to redesign the way his entire crew interacted. He had to design a new genetic code that focused on unleashing the passion and commitment of his crew rather than having them passively wait for an order. In keeping with our genetics metaphor, these interactions come from three genes.

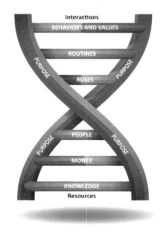

Designing the Genetic Circuitry that
Links Resources with Purpose

The Genetic Code of Rules. Most organizations have too many meaningless, valueless, and, frankly, stupid rules. The worst are the unwritten rules, the evolutionary byproduct of years of neglecting mission critical objectives. In designing the DNA of this new leadership system, Marquet tossed out a few old rules and designed a few new ones to engage the workforce.

One of Marquet's new rules challenged the traditional model of a leader as a great problem solver. Marquet designed a radically different rule, "Resist the urge to provide solutions."[3] This may sound odd from a man who graduated top of his class at the United States Naval Academy. Yet I will be introducing you to an award-winning healthcare organization that also requires leaders to *avoid solving* problems for their staff.

Solving a problem for a worker who is perfectly capable of solving it themselves only serves to maintain the manager's power. Delegating problem solving increases the workforce's value and confidence. By contrast, managers who solve problems can be seen as disrespectful of their workforce's intelligence and robbing workers of the opportunity to grow and develop problem-solving skills.

The Genetic Code of Routines. In his book, Marquet recounts a story of shutting down the nuclear reactor and hooking the submarine up to 440-volt shore power. Obviously, this is a technical and potentially dangerous activity. A clear process was in place with safety checks along the way, but still, a mistake happened. In reviewing the error, the usual suspects came up, "mistakes are sometimes unavoidable, we need better training," etc. But, as in other organizations I researched, Marquet used this accident as a learning opportunity for the entire

3 Meadows, Donella H. *Thinking in Systems: A Primer*. Chelsea Green Publishing, 2008. Kindle Edition. Kindle Location 941.

crew. The result was a new routine called "take deliberate action." This routine required the sailor to pause and vocalize what he was about to do before doing it. This process became what Charles Duhigg, in his book *The Power of Habit*, calls a keystone habit.

Routines are institutional muscle memory. "Take deliberate action" became a new routine that forced sailors to slow down so they would not go on "autopilot," something that could be deadly when cruising at depths that could crush the submarine in seconds. The following words, attributed to Aristotle, reflect this sentiment. "We are what we repeatedly do. Excellence, then, is not an act, but a habit."

The Genetic Code of Behaviors. One surprising discovery I made was how seriously high-performing organizations take their leaders' personal behavior and tie their behaviors to the workforce's experience. Furthermore, they codify proper behaviors into various versions of a charter.

The *USS Santa Fe* was no different. Marquet and his officers developed a list of "Guiding Principles" that clearly defined behavioral expectations for officers and sailors. Things like initiative, courage, commitment, integrity, and empowerment were required. These principles were wisely developed by the entire crew, so everyone had input.

Results

The result was an entirely new way of leading the crew of the *Santa Fe*. Instead of one captain giving orders to 134 sailors, Captain Marquet turned this around and created a system where all 135 sailors were fully engaged and intellectually and emotionally committed to the submarine's success. Two years after implementing this system, the *USS Santa Fe* received the "highest grade anyone had ever seen on our reactor operations examination, with top marks in every area."[4] All this happened without firing anyone. In both performance and morale, the *Santa Fe* had risen from worst to first. Furthermore, the system, like your DNA and mine, replicated itself. Over the next ten years, ten *Santa Fe* officers were selected to command submarines, five became squadron commanders (or the equivalent), and so far, two have become admirals.[5]

In upcoming chapters, you will see how other high-performing organizations designed systems of leadership around this same system structure. In doing so, they catapulted themselves from average or worse, to elite levels of long-term performance.

---

4 Marquet, L. David. *Turn the Ship Around!* New York, NY: Penguin Publishing Group. Kindle Edition, 2012. Kindle location 1894.
5 https://www.youtube.com/watch?v=eVhu4OsfvOs. Accessed May 18, 2020.

LEADERSHIP DEBRIEF AND EXERCISES

Do the following exercise on index cards or Post-it notes.

1. How do you think the crew of the *USS Santa Fe* felt experiencing Captain Marquet's brand of leadership? Record one idea per card and use a minimum of three, but no more than five, cards.

2. What kind of daily experience would motivate you to fully engage with your organization? What would make you wildly passionate about going to work every day? Write down one idea per card, using a minimum of three, but no more than five, cards.

3. If you are already a leader or an emerging leader, ask yourself candidly, "What kind of experience do I offer others?" Or, "What is the experience of my staff from my leadership?" Does the experience you describe line up with number one above?

4. Now, repeat the exercise based on your team.

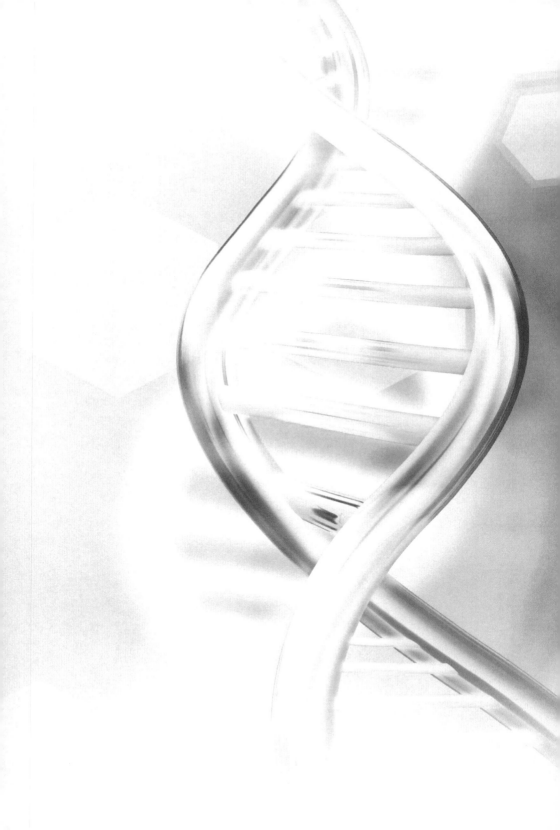

SECTION 1

LEVERAGING THE POWER OF PURPOSE OR OUTCOME

"The least obvious part of the system, its function or purpose, is often the most crucial determinate of the system's behavior."

— Donella Meadows, *Thinking in Systems: A Primer*

Right now, as I am writing these words, or right now, as you are reading them, eleven fully integrated systems are keeping us alive and well. They include the circulatory system, the digestive system, the endocrine system, and the reproductive system. Each system is self-monitoring, each has an output that is required by the other ten, and each fully supports and is supported by the other ten. Remove one and the body either stops functioning or is severally compromised.

For example, the circulatory system delivers nutrients and gases to the muscular system so we can take a walk or train as an Olympic athlete. Socially and organizationally, we live in a world of interlocking systems. Each system produces something unique and distinctive while supporting a larger system. Organizations operate with financial systems, HR systems, operational systems, and sales and marketing systems. Ideally, each is integrated with the others while producing a purpose necessary for the entire organization's success.

This book will argue that leadership itself is not only one of these systems, but the most important system of all. As I noted with Captain Marquet and his design of a new system of leadership that turned around the lowest-performing submarine in the US Navy, the most critical component of that system was the purpose. Metaphorically, Marquet's intent that his crew of 135 sailors would all be psychologically and emotionally engaged became the two sides of the DNA molecule. It became the backbone of the system. Genetically, the backbone provides DNA's basic structure and explains how it can be six feet long but still fit into an individual human cell. For a system of leadership, the outcome is what builds the employee experience, turns the workforce into ambassadors, and drives customer value. It also drives innovation and transformation.

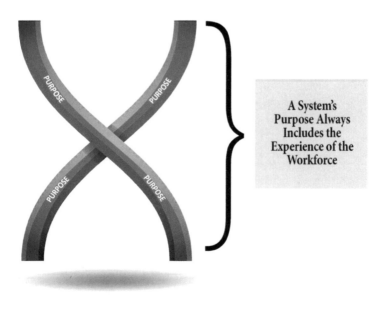

A System's
Purpose Always
Includes the
Experience of the
Workforce

***

No other organization in the world takes leadership as seriously as the US military, and specifically for our purposes, the US Army. As part of my research, I interviewed two senior officers. One was Four-Star General Barry McCaffrey, one of the most highly decorated generals to have ever worn the uniform. Upon his retirement, he became Director of the Office of National Drug Control Policy for President Clinton. During our interview, he was clear: "The US Army practices servant leadership." In virtually the same breath, he also mentioned love—a word I was not expecting to hear from a certified war hero and recipient of multiple purple hearts. Yet he spoke openly and candidly about being loved by a superior officer, General "Stormin'" Norman Schwarzkopf, commander of the United States Central Command, who led coalition forces in the first Gulf War.

Service and love? His exact words were, "He (Schwarzkopf) actually loved me."

Frankly, I was stunned. I was not expecting to hear something so intimate and intensely personal. I wondered if this might have been just a personal perspective. Turns out love and service are built into the DNA of US Army officer training.

On September 8, 2009, Captain William Swenson was part of an operation of 106 US and Afghan forces operating in the Ganjgal Valley in the Eastern Kunar Province of Afghanistan. They were making their way up the valley to meet with senior leaders of a village thought to be friendly to US and Afghan forces. It was a setup. About 6:00 a.m., they were ambushed by a superior Taliban force. The troops were taking fire from the front and both sides of the valley. They were outnumbered and outgunned. The fighting was so close and intense that the Taliban offered the US and Afghan forces the opportunity to surrender. In response, Swenson threw them a live hand grenade.

US and Afghan forces were taking casualties. Sergeant First Class Kenneth Westbrook was severely wounded, shot in the neck, bleeding, and lying in the open. In an act of personal courage, Swenson ran across the field of fire and pulled Westbrook to safety. In a viral video,[6] Swenson is seen carrying Westbrook to a helicopter, helping him inside, and before going back to retrieve more wounded, giving the sergeant a kiss on the side of his head. Two weeks later, Sergeant First Class Kenneth Westbrook died from his wounds. Swenson received the nation's highest award for valor—the Medal of Honor.

While Swenson's personal courage should never be discounted, it could also be argued that the genetic code to which he had been trained kicked in and he responded to his primary role or purpose as an Army officer—to love and serve subordinates. Sounds...religious. But love in the US Army? The Army trains soldiers to kill, yet it also trains leaders, instilling a set of core values, modifying their DNA, if you will. One core value is Selfless Service, defined as "putting the welfare of the nation, the Army, and your subordinates before your own."

Is there a better way to describe love than putting others' welfare above your own? What the Army has done is build love and service into its system of leadership. These twin values form the backbone of the Army's double helix. In its leadership training, it has scaled it up so that all 1.3 million active duty personnel and 700,000 reservists are trained to the same code.

Creating the Employee Experience

When I started this project, I was not thinking of the employee experience or company brand. Yet every time I found an intentional

---

6 https://www.youtube.com/watch?v=eVhu4OsfvOs. Accessed May 18, 2020.

leadership system, I also found a robust employee experience. When General McCaffrey spoke of servant leadership, he was talking about a methodology, and when he spoke of love, it was the result of leaders serving those they lead. You might be wondering if this was just a statement from a personal perspective. As it turns out, I heard the exact same thing from another senior member of the US Army.

One of my earliest interviews was with Colonel Marc Gauthier. He was a thirty-four-year veteran and Army Ranger who served mostly with the Special Forces. He was candid about servant leadership and how his priority was to care for those under him. He spoke of loving his soldiers and how difficult it was to see them going into harm's way during deployments in Iraq, knowing some might not return. Unfortunately for me, I somewhat discounted his perspective because he served in the Chaplaincy. I thought "of course he should serve and love those he served with; he is a chaplain." However, after my interview with General McCaffrey, an officer who holds multiple Purple Hearts and has lead men into combat, I realized both officers were telling me the same story—the purpose of an Army officer is to serve those they lead. When they do this, they end up loving those under their command/leadership/care. This is an extraordinarily high calling. Does the Army serve and love soldiers perfectly? Of course not.

In the next four chapters, you will discover four different organizations and the purpose of their system of leadership. In the first chapter, I will introduce a manufacturing organization that focuses on servant leadership and employee engagement. In the next, we will look at a Native American healthcare system that focuses on relationships, which fits its unique worldview. The third chapter is about a multinational manufacturing firm that focuses on employee safety. While each organization is different, one could argue all three end up in the same place—taking care of those they lead. This observation is accurate, but each took an approach unique to them and the kind of organization they wanted to create.

In the fourth chapter, I will introduce an iconic healthcare organization that took its eye off its transcendent purpose to focus on revenues. The result was catastrophic.

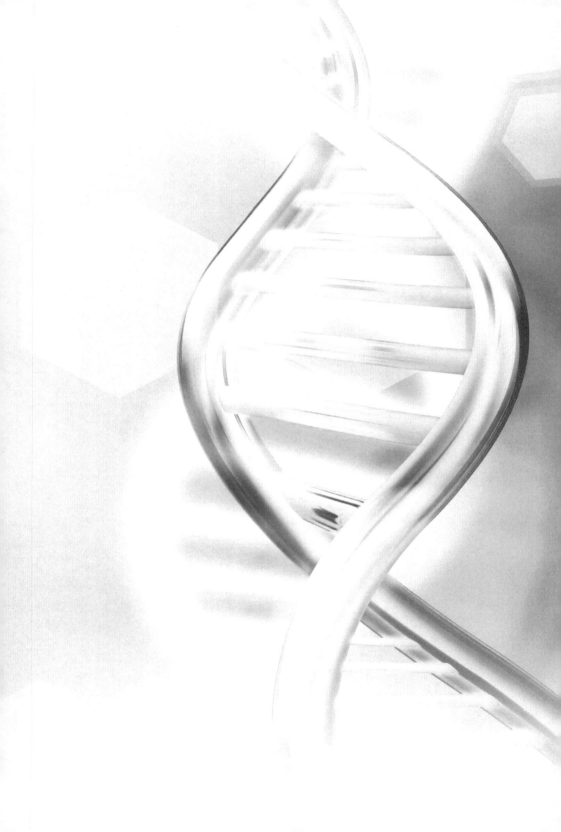

CHAPTER 1

LEVERAGING THE PURPOSE OF SERVICE AND ENGAGEMENT

"If you want to go fast, go alone. If you want to go far, go together."

— African Proverb

At approximately 8:00 a.m. all around the world, people arrive at work. A few are getting off. Some are looking forward to their day. About half understand their jobs as a means to pay the bills, buy the groceries, and put their kids through college. Other than that, their jobs or employers mean little to them. Most of them are looking for a new job at any given moment. A few more, 13 percent according to Gallup, are angry with their managers and would love to get out from under their control.

However, in a few organizations, employees are actually looking forward to their day. Maybe an idea struck them last night as they were going to sleep about how to save time and money, streamline a process, improve the workflow, or create a new feature that customers have been talking about. They can't wait to share their idea with their team because they know if it is a good idea, or an idea their team can improve upon, their manager will acknowledge and support them.

Servant leadership is a philosophy that says the best leaders serve the workforce. They look out for the welfare of their subordinates. They willingly share power and help those they serve grow. It is a nice idea a lot of people talk and write about, but few know how to implement it.

In a conversation I had with a senior executive of an international non-profit, she joked that she'd had a supervisor who understood servant leadership as serving the coffee at the Monday morning staff meetings. "The rest of the week, he just acted like a jerk."

Mostly, servant leadership is seen as being a nice boss. However, the US Marine Corps and the US Army have infused servant leadership into officer training and development. Other organizations have discovered how to implement servant leadership, as well. They engineer it like designer DNA and build it into their leadership and management systems.

***

Kaas Tailored is at the south end of Paine Field, near Everett, Washington. They design and manufacture custom commercial and retail furniture. Their customers include major aerospace, fashion, retail, healthcare, and hospitality companies. Most of their customers have been with them for years, even decades. Want to do business with them? Get in line. They are as picky about their customers as they are about quality control. They are so good that in the last six years, 40,000 people have toured their facilities to learn what they are doing. Like the US Army, they, too, understand servant leadership as a path to an engaged workforce.

Kaas Tailored was launched in the late 1970s. In 1998, Jeff Kaas, the son of one of the founders, became president. Not long after, his largest and most prestigious customer, a major aerospace firm, came to him and said, "Jeff, we are concerned about cost. We want you to adopt Lean." (Lean is the Americanized term frequently used to describe *kaizen*. *Kaizen* is a Japanese word meaning improvement.)

Kaas' first reaction was, "What's Lean?"

It proved to be a life-changing question.

Over the next ten years, Jeff and his team traveled to Japan several times to see how Toyota built cars and attempted to apply what they saw. By 2006, they had learned enough to know Lean or *kaizen* worked, but their results were limited. Jeff explained that they were treating it like a manufacturing technique, not an integrated operational and management system. To take the next step, they had to get serious about waste and extracting it wherever and whenever it showed up. He also had to take a different approach to leadership that required him to care for his customers *and* for his workers and their families. As Jeff said, "I had to determine—did I give a shit?"

For example, Jeff had a nice office, befitting a company CEO, but it was clear it was a waste of real estate. It was also a two-lane tunnel through which six lanes of daily problems and decisions became compressed and delayed as they were prioritized and eventually responded to. This situation made Jeff and his office the cause of a traffic jam that slowed growth, improvement, and innovation. Today, no offices are in the complex that houses Kaas Tailored. A visitor will only find Jeff out on the production floor, coaching and mentoring the workforce.

Kaas Tailored is fanatical about eliminating waste. Every leader, production lead, coach, and mentor is trained in *kaizen*. However, they do not just "do" *kaizen*; they practice it daily. *Kaizen* has been coded into the genetics, the DNA of their integrated system of leadership and management. Consequently, with 200 employees, the workforce (not just managers and leaders) initiates 1,000 to 1,250 *kaizens*—improvements—each year. On average, each *kaizen* generates $1,000 of savings annually or the equivalent of 4 to 5 percent of gross sales every year.

In addition, employees are equally rewarded if they do *kaizen* for Kaas or do a personal *kaizen*. Jeff wants his employees to understand *kaizen* and practice it so it becomes part of their operating DNA. Consequently, he rewards his employees with PTO (personal time off) even if the *kaizen* is purely personal.

Jeff's passion for eliminating waste goes deeper than improving his bottom line. From my observation, it is about rewarding, recognizing, and unleashing the human capacity for creativity and innovation.

During my tour of Kaas Tailored's facilities, I listened as a woman who had only been with Kaas a few months described how she had identified an opportunity to get five parts out of the same amount of foam core material from which they had been getting four parts. In her very personal story, she described seeing this opportunity and going to her mentor to see if it was a good idea. Her mentor then coached her through the *kaizen* process—how to submit, test, and then implement her idea. I noticed that every time she used the term mentor, she would turn toward a quiet woman standing next to her. I finally had to ask the obvious question, "Is this woman your supervisor?" She looked at me a bit bewildered and said, "Well, I guess so, but we just call them mentors."

In designing his leadership system, Jeff abolished the traditional role of leader as traffic cop and redefined it. At Kaas Tailored, leaders are trained in mentoring and coaching their staff. Leaders are the primary support for front-line staff in the battle to find and eliminate waste.

At the end of my tour, during a short debrief, I asked if they had an overriding purpose to their leadership. Todd, the production manager, stood up, deliberately stepped toward me, squared his shoulders, looked at me directly, and said, "We practice servant leadership."

Servant leadership is a philosophy as much as it is a model. Philosophically, servant leaders focus on developing the workforce, sharing power, coaching, mentoring, and supporting front line staff in their service to the customer or patient. While it could have been called many things, it was clear Jeff and his team had designed and developed an integrated system of leadership and management that empowered the entire workforce. This system comes with a complete genetic code that is hardwired into how they serve their customers, employees, and community.

Servant leadership also forced Jeff to make some difficult decisions. Did servant leadership mean he had to care about the whole person he hired, or could he segregate people into parts and just care about those bits that contributed to his business? I believe it takes enormous courage to say, "I care about the whole person walking in the door, as opposed to just the parts I can use."

As Kaas Tailored grew and the staff became skilled at *kaizen*, Jeff was faced with a dilemma. Local manufacturing firms who could pay more started hiring his best people. Would he support members of his team if they grew and then left for a greater opportunity, or would he put up barriers, fighting to keep his well-trained employees? Turns out Jeff cannot separate personal from professional values. Consequently, Jeff actively trains and prepares his staff for bigger and better opportunities that may arise so they will be ready to jump at the chance.

In my conversation with Jeff, he recounted a sad, but all-too-prevalent story. He is frequently invited to speak with business groups and companies interested in adopting *kaizen*. He had recently visited with senior leadership at a large financial firm. His first question to them was, "How much time do you and your staff spend on activities that add little to no value to your customers?" The response was typical: around

40 to 50 percent. He asked, "What is your average work week—you and your employees?" Again, the response was typical: around fifty to sixty hours a week. Then Jeff asked, "How can you ask your employees to sacrifice time with their family and friends, so the company can flush it down the toilet on work that has no value?"

After a bit, he said, "Do you give a shit?"

They did not. Talking about care for employees and maximizing customer value is one thing. Doing it takes work. For too many leaders with a short-term view, it is just easier to kick the hard work back to the next administration.

However, Jeff's purpose of servant leadership requires him to care. Metaphorically, Jeff Kaas wants to build one of those giant sequoia trees—a tree that will live a long time. A tree that will withstand the hurricanes of economic markets and seasons of drought, fire, and flood. But those beautiful trees don't just grow tall and strong because their DNA says they should. Their leaves are especially good at capturing moisture from fog, collecting it, and then releasing it so the larger environment can benefit from this water. Jeff wants Kaas Tailored to be this kind of company. A kind of company that provides opportunities and growth to all who fall under its canopy. And in case you are wondering, Kaas Tailored is a highly profitable company. Choosing servant leadership does not conflict with financial goals. It generates dividends that grow and compound.

Debrief

Research into the likes and mannerisms of millennials tells us, in the workplace, they are not interested in bosses. They do, however, want coaches. Having raised a millennial myself and observed his generation, this makes perfectly good sense to me. All millennials' lives, older adults have reached out to them. My son Jason has been studying karate for twenty-two years and has just received his fourth-degree black belt. Throughout these years, his sanseis (teachers) have been mentors and coaches, not authoritarian bosses. Even in his first job out of high school, Jason was coached and mentored in the discipline and practice of selling high-end kitchen cutlery.

Jeff's system of dropping traditional management roles and turning them into coaches and mentors serving those they lead seems ideal for attracting and retaining millennials. Furthermore, it is a system that emerging leaders, millennials or not, can easily learn. We will see in following sections that his approach to training puts zero value on traditional classroom-based training. It is all about coaching and mentoring.

Servant leadership and the resulting emphasis on coaching and mentoring is more than a value that gets turned into a decorative poster for the lunchroom. Jeff built it into the DNA of Kaas Tailored's leadership.

Emerging leaders can use this tool by starting with a clear purpose and knowing what kind of leadership they want their staff to experience. This builds your organization's employee brand.

Jeff wants every employee to feel they have a voice and can contribute to the company's success. He does this through servant leadership and trains his leaders to do the same. Is it the only way? Absolutely not. But this system is building the employee experience at Kaas Tailored. They don't have to publicize it or post it on their website. The word gets around that Kaas is a place where workers are respected and their voices are valued. They are rewarded for speaking up. Maybe that is why the first thing I noticed when I walked into their facilities was that everyone was smiling.

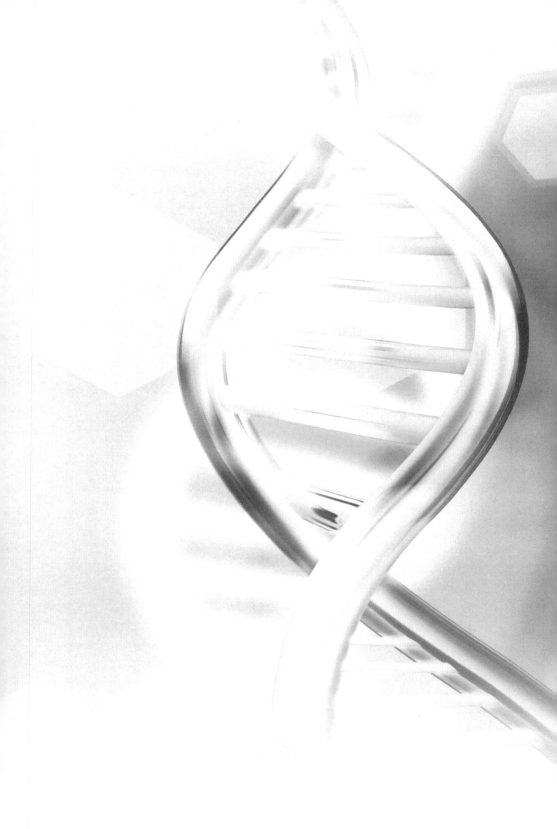

CHAPTER 2

LEVERAGING THE PURPOSE OF RELATIONSHIP

"Nuka = strong, giant structures and living things."

— Alaskan Native Term

In the last chapter, I introduced a design and manufacturing company that set servant leadership and employee engagement as the purpose, or output, of its leadership system. Kaas Tailored took this approach because Jeff Kaas felt it was the company's best opportunity to achieve its mission, not because he was personally good at it. I think he would say he is learning servant leadership right alongside the rest of his team.

In contrast, I have spoken with many leaders who feel their ability to develop relationships is central to their leadership style. It is usually their strength, so, of course, they focus on it. Genetically, we are hard-wired to need relationships. However, in North America, we are also in love with our individuality, which means we tend to believe in the myth of the lone genius—the leader who will bring us to the promised land of corporate success.

Brian is a young man and brilliant civil engineer. He is a millennial leading his firm's initiatives using virtual reality to design large public construction projects. In his early thirties, he applied for an internal promotion. The job placed him among 300 others leading one of the world's largest engineering firms. As he explained, "I thought I was ap-plying for a title. Then they gave it to me, and I realized I had no clue what I was supposed to do as a leader."

Brian had substantial experience managing the design and construction of large hydraulic projects. But managing multiple teams with different engineering skills, across multiple markets, geographically dispersed, was...different. He had to lead—something for which he was not trained. In the absence of corporate direction, he did what he was trained to do—he built a system, only this one was a leadership system.

It is difficult to understand how an international firm with $5 billion in revenues could not spare a dime to ensure Brian was a successful leader. Unfortunately, this is the norm. Brian was lucky because he is by nature a systems thinker. He modeled his system after his personal values (exactly what most people do). Brian is Christian, so he studied what Jesus taught about leadership. Then he read several best-selling books on leadership. His research led him to conclude that leadership is fundamentally a "relational enterprise." Therefore, his personal leadership had to produce *relationships* if his teams were going to succeed.

Brian described to me a series of simple routines he initiated to build relationships. These routines became part of his leadership DNA, the genetic code that determines how he personally leads. This code also included a 360-degree evaluation of his leadership. When I asked about the results, he said, "I had to close the door to my office because I was crying. I had no idea how meaningful it was to my staff to have a relationship with me." He then added, "I am the youngest (thirty-seven) of these 300 senior leaders. The next youngest is ten years my senior, but the crazy thing is, they are asking me how to lead."

This is the good news about Brian. The bad news for his firm is 299 leaders are muddling through this thing called leadership. A few will do well through natural gifts and talent. A few more will eventually figure it out. A few will drown in the process. But what will this muddling through cost the staff, stakeholders, and customers? Unfortunately, the cost will never show up as a budgetary line item. Yet it is a major expense that is costing them millions.

If relationships are important to business outcomes, and the workforce having authentic relationships with their managers is key to engagement and sustainability, the only way to capture this is to scale it to the entire organization with a system designed with that intent. The following case will demonstrate the power of a comprehensive system of organizational leadership designed to intentionally produce relationships.

***

For Alaskan Natives, relationships are how they have survived. Individual members rely on the tribe, however dispersed it may be. Tribal community is built into their cultural DNA. This idea of relationship is at the core of their identity, their story. Oral histories have kept their cultures alive for thousands of years, and telling stories is how they connect the past with the present to understand their history. Storytelling is how they retain their identity.

It should be no surprise that an Alaskan Native healthcare organization adopted relationships and stories as the philosophical core of how they deliver medical care. Relationships and stories are how they bring healing to individual patients, but also to their families and communities. This is their story—and it is a very successful one.

In 1741, a Dutch explorer named Vitus Johansson Bering was the first European to set eyes on Alaska. Voyages by Russian, British, Spanish, and French explorers soon followed. The Russians quickly recognized and exploited Alaska's economic opportunities. With the Chinese paying more for otter pelts than their weight in gold, fur traders quickly established trading outposts. The first was in 1784 on Kodiak Island.

Foreign traders were not very good at hunting otter, but indigenous populations were, and soon, Russian traders began to enslave the indigenous population in their lust for furs. Families were ripped apart when women were given to Russian traders for their own pleasure. European diseases, from which indigenous populations had no immunity, wiped out entire villages. In the eyes of the world, Russia came to own Alaska.

In 1867, Russia sold Alaska to the US for $7.2 million. It was dubbed "Seward's Folly" because voters could not conceive any value in the desolate cold of Alaska. But in 1896, gold was discovered in the Yukon. A massive new wave of traders (miners and prospectors) invaded Alaska. In the lower forty-eight states, the government tried putting indigenous peoples on reservations to control them. The result was successive waves of uprisings and massacres.

In Alaska, the US government focused on assimilating the 231 federally recognized Alaskan tribes into mainstream (white) culture. Consequently, children were prohibited from speaking their native languages in school. Traditional spiritual and cultural ceremonies were prohibited or discouraged. The result was the legal loss of self-determination, one of the most fundamental values of the Declaration of Independence, the United States Constitution, and the Bill of Rights, and the breakdown of traditional family and social customs, which was followed by despair, widespread alcoholism and addiction, domestic abuse, and violence.

Two years after gold was discovered in the Yukon, the United States colonized the Philippines. This gave Filipinos the right to migrate to the western shores of the US in search of better lives. The first immigrants were young men looking for opportunity. Many found work in the agricultural fields of Hawaii, California, Oregon, and Washington and in the salmon canneries of Alaska. Though conditions were often deplorable, a robust and thriving fishing industry meant steady work.

Katherine Gottlieb's mother is an Alaskan Native and her father is Filipino. She was raised not far from Kodiak Island, the site of that first Russian trading outpost. She is one of twelve children, and once she was old enough, she worked to help support her brothers and sisters. One of those early jobs was in a crab cannery. When she married and started raising her own children, she and her family moved to Anchorage, and she continued to work in the canneries.

The cannery managers liked Gottlieb because she was fast. She had a passion for efficiency and a certain feistiness that won her the respect of her employers. Eventually, she would go back to school to study for her GED. Then she began work on her associate's degree. This was followed up with a bachelor's degree and an MBA from Alaska Pacific University. Later, Alaska Pacific University would also award her an honorary doctorate. While she was working on her associate degree, Gottlieb applied for a job at the newly formed Southcentral Foundation (SCF), a fledging healthcare organization with a budget of $3 million and twenty-four employees. Gottlieb's education qualified her to be a receptionist, but when she was asked about her long-term career objectives, she said she wanted to be the CEO. Four years later, her wish came true: she was named CEO.

SCF was formed as a result of the Indian Self-Determination and Education Assistance Act of 1975. This Act reversed decades of attempted assimilation. It allowed the federal government to contract directly with tribal organizations for, among other things, tribal healthcare. It gave indigenous peoples some measure of self-determination. Prior to this time, healthcare was controlled by Washington, DC, 4,200 miles to the southeast. It was expensive, inefficient, and disconnected from indigenous values, culture, and customers.

Founded in 1982, the SCF was formed under the tribal authority of Cook Inlet Region, Inc., to provide healthcare and related services to Alaskan Native and American Indian peoples. Initially, services were basic dentistry, optometry, etc. In 1998, the federal government transferred responsibility for the healthcare of 200 Alaskan Native tribes into the hands of SCF. It was an historic event.

When SCF was given the opportunity to serve these tribes, Gottlieb and her team immediately began a philosophical overhaul that celebrated traditional values in collaboration with Western medicine. The overhaul had two major components: 1) terminology (the term patients was too passive and was replaced with "customer-owners"), and 2) story and relationship. Part story and part relationship is how Alaskan Natives understand spirituality. They see life as a connected whole rather than a series of parts. Therefore, spirituality is incorporated into delivering care. Where Western medicine ignores, if not outright scorns, spirituality, SCF celebrates it. Just outside the Alaska Native Medical Center is a traditional herb garden that grows forty-five different herbs and medicinal plants used in Alaskan Native healing and spiritual rituals. While the hospital does not dispense these to customer-owners, they will teach them how to use the plants. This is a small but important part of a total system of care that puts the customer-owners in charge of their own health. It gives them self-determination. To ignore indigenous people's sense of spirituality is to devalue their culture and customs. It devalues their story. However, by celebrating spirituality, SCF builds trust, respect, and relationship.

By 2017, SCF was providing care to nearly 66,000 customer-owners spread across 200 tribes. This represents 100 percent of the Native Americans living in its geographical footprint, which stretches 107,400 square miles across Southcentral Alaska. The eastern border is Canada, and the western border is the end of the Aleutian chain and the Pribilof Islands in the Bering Sea. It employs 2,200 staff, including physician/providers, and has an annual operating budget of nearly $350 million.

At virtually every level, SCF's performance ranks with the nation's best.

- Top 25 percent for clinical measures
- Top 10 percent financial sustainability
- Patient satisfaction scores at 96 percent
- Awarded their first Malcolm Baldrige National Quality Award in 2011
- Awarded their second Malcolm Baldrige National Quality Award in 2017

A Malcolm Baldrige National Quality Award is the nation's highest award for performance excellence and quality in the healthcare, business, education, and nonprofit sectors. To win it once is a monumental achievement. To win it twice is a distinction very few organizations have ever achieved.

Don Berwick, former Administrator for the Centers for Medicare and Medicaid Services (CMS) under the Obama Administration, said of SCF, "I think it's the leading example of healthcare redesign in the nation, maybe the world."[7] SCF has become so good at delivering healthcare that they now consult and train healthcare providers from around the world.

---

7 https://www.youtube.com/watch?v=gg0qUCx9A68&feature=youtu.be. Accessed May 21, 2020.

Gottlieb is proud to explain that they have a name for their approach: the Nuka System of Care. Nuka is an Alaskan Native word for strong, giant structures and living things. Like everything strong and living, it comes with DNA, a genetic code that makes it strong and alive. SCF leadership's genetic code is engineered to build relationships. Through the power of relationships, they are not only treating symptoms, they are healing whole families and communities.

Debrief

Gallup reports that millennials want jobs they can emotionally and behaviorally connect with. They are seeking a life of purpose that is healthy with a good work-life balance. In my own conversations with millennials, I am impressed by the way they want their lives to be integrated. They expect to integrate their personal missions, callings, and values with their work. Frankly, I find this refreshing. They don't want to live by one set of values at work, another set at home, and a third set in their community. This worldview is distinctive to this generation, and employers must understand this if they are going to build a strong employee experience that will attract millennials.

Brian and SCF's stories provide two important lessons:

First, if you are an emerging leader starting your first management job, don't expect much in the way of training or coaching. If some training is offered, take it but don't expect too much from it. Even if it is the best leadership training on the planet, there is a high probability the existing system of leadership within your organization will make it difficult, if not impossible, to implement. Like Brian, you may have to design your own system. Brian shows it can be done and done very effectively. He serves as a model, but the most important thing we learn from Brian and SCF is to lead *toward* a purpose. This is different than leading with a purpose. Both Brian and SCF's objective is to systematically lead in such a way that relationship is the result. It is the output of their system.

Second, for the seasoned executive, know that millennials who are emerging as leaders or potential leaders are better educated and smarter than you were when you were the same age. You can allow them all to develop their own systems or have the foresight to design one for the entire organization and tap into the power of designed systems. This is what SCF did, and as a result, they are building a worldwide reputation in healthcare delivery to indigenous peoples.

In the next chapter, we will see how employee safety was used to engage the entire workforce of an international industrial giant. The result was not only employee safety, but industry-leading economic performance.

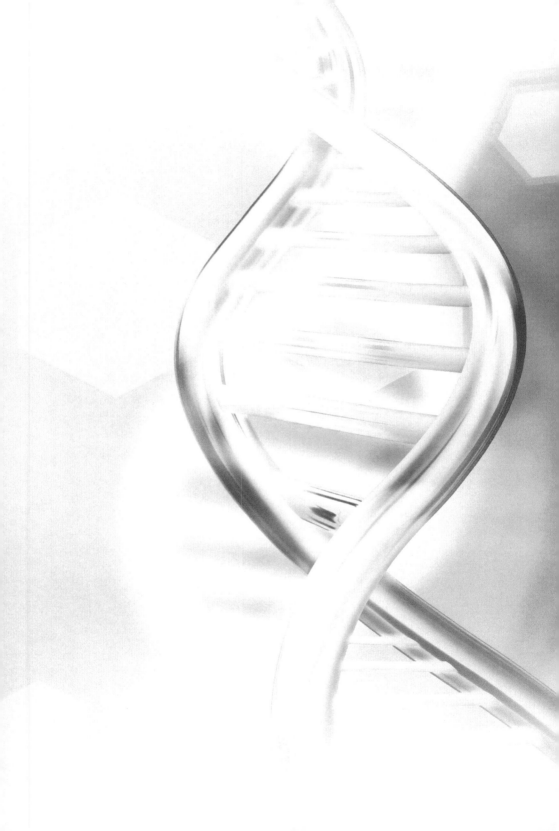

CHAPTER 3

LEVERAGING THE PURPOSE OF EMPLOYEE SAFETY

"Common Statement of Belief: 'Our most important
asset is our people.' There's damn little evidence that
it's true...It's just a syrupy sentiment."

— Paul O'Neil

Servant leadership, employee engagement, relationship, and story—each is a purpose seen with clarity through the eyes and experience of the workforce. The danger for many organizations is in thinking the purpose of leadership is lowering costs and raising the quality of their "widgets" (whatever their "product" is). This means that, all too often, the value of the workforce is measured by production. This measurement tends to devalue human ingenuity and creativity. People become good at/for one thing, putting round pegs into round holes. The human capacity for service, innovation, and creativity—the most valuable parts—can be left at the door.

There is a lot of talk these days about the need for frank communication, a willingness to be open and honest about failure, and a commitment to vulnerability. These are all wonderful goals on a personal level. But the challenge is to scale these values organizationally so they become part of the organizational DNA. I like the way Ed Catmull describes the process of the brain trust at Pixar: "Frank talk, spirited debate, laughter, and love."[8]

8 Catmull, Ed and Amy Wallace. *Creativity, Inc.: Overcoming the Unseen Forces That Stand in the Way of True Inspiration*. New York, NY: Random House

Pixar has institutionalized the values of open communication, or what it calls candor. Could other words be used in place of candor? Certainly, but the word has special meaning and significance to an organization whose life blood depends on artistic and technical creativity. For Pixar, candor has become a gene in its DNA. But open communication can take many forms. No form is always the best one. Each organization can find its own way of embracing open and honest communication and do so in ways that are meaningful and valuable to them.

*****

The following is a story of two highly respected CEOs who designed two very different systems of leadership to create two very different organizations.

Paul O'Neil and Jack Welch were born less than three weeks apart in 1935, during the grueling days of the Great Depression. Both went to college and earned advanced degrees. Jack earned a PhD in chemical engineering. After studying economics, Paul earned a Master's in public administration. Both are numbers men. They are strong believers in data and the power of numbers to tell a story. Both rose to become highly respected CEOs of well-known industrial giants, which they helped to achieve unparalleled economic performance. Other than these similarities, the two men could not be more different.

Jack Welch became the CEO of General Electric in 1981 and retired in 2001. In 1999, *Fortune* magazine named Jack "Manager of the Century." His strategy for growing GE was based on divesting underperforming business units and people while investing in growing areas. During his tenure, he was famous for believing every GE business had to be number one or two in the world. His nickname, "Neutron Jack,"
Publishing Group. Kindle Edition, 2014. Kindle Locations 1577-1590.

was a reference to the neutron bomb, which kills people but leaves buildings intact. In those days, symbolic "public hangings" of managers who failed to meet expectations were commonplace. In his wake, Jack left behind a very profitable company based on a culture of fear.

As of 2019, GE is still struggling to come out from under Jack Welch's shadow and recapture innovation. Beth Comstock, the former Vice Chair of GE, in an interview explained her method of combating a culture of fear was to blame the manager and pass out permission slips. Really? One of the most powerful positions in one of the world's most powerful companies, and her approach to a culture of fear that stifled innovation was to pass out permission slips? Instead of passing out permission slips, she should have worked to design a system that took fear out of the workforce experience. In 2018, after 110 years, GE was delisted from the Dow Jones Industrial Average.

Paul O'Neil was born in St. Louis, Missouri. He met his wife in high school. They would marry and have four children, twelve grandchildren, and (at last report) nine great-grandchildren. Paul loved lists and had a mind for analytics. After university, he started out as a middle manager in the Veterans Administration but was quickly recognized for his analytical skills and recruited to what we now call the Office of Management and Budget (OMB). By the time he was thirty-eight, Paul was the deputy director. He had a reputation for asking a lot of questions and getting to the root cause of problems—skills he would take to the private sector.

After a few years with International Paper, Paul was selected to become CEO of Alcoa Aluminum. It was an unusual appointment for a successful bureaucrat. Alcoa, at the time, was a mess. Quality was poor. Labor was unhappy. The unions protested unfair labor practices, making picket lines commonplace. Paul was replacing a long-time

CEO, and many executives were angry they had been passed over in favor of an outsider, and a government outsider at that. Paul's selection as CEO was met with more than a little skepticism.

Paul was introduced to Wall Street in October 1987. The usual crowd was there: major investors, market analysts, and a few reporters. These kinds of events have a familiar script. First the chairman of the board or some executive introduces the new CEO, who then gets up and talks about the company's legacy and how its best years are in front of it. Then the CEO becomes part of the company "us" by talking about "them"—government and its regulations, which are especially hard on whichever industry is doing the talking. Then the CEO throws in a few words about market expansion, cost reduction, and maybe a word or two about quality. These events are designed to make Wall Street comfortable, rather than create controversy.

On the day of his introduction, Paul O'Neil looked very much like a CEO. He was slim, with silver-white hair; he was confident and articulate. Then he began to speak. His first words were: "I want to talk to you about worker safety. Every year numerous Alcoa workers are injured so badly that they miss a day of work...."[9] He said nothing about market expansion, government regulation, quality, or productivity.

Alcoa already had good safety numbers—better than all the national averages. However, Paul wanted to eliminate injuries completely. And he wanted to do this in places where 2,000-degree (F) molten aluminum was being turned into everything from soda cans to airplane wings with machinery that could rip a person in two. When he said worker safety would be his top priority, he got everyone's attention, but not in a good way. One Wall Street analyst, upon hearing this rad-

9 Duhigg, Charles. *The Power of Habit.* New York, NY: Random House, 2012. p. 98. Kindle location 1555.

ical and unconventional approach to company growth, sprinted to the phone and told his investors to sell their shares because "The board put a crazy hippie in charge, and he's going to kill the company."[10] Later, the analyst said it was the worst advice he ever gave his clients.

Six months after Paul took over, disaster struck. A young man, new to the company and about to become a first-time father, was killed when an aluminum extrusion press jammed. Determined to free the press, he went inside a safety zone (a place a worker only enters when specific safety protocols are in place) as two managers watched. When he freed the jammed press, a six-foot arm resumed its arc, crushing his skull. He died instantly. After reviewing videotapes and recreating the accident through diagrams, Paul announced to all of Alcoa's plant executives: "We killed this man."

Paul did not single out individuals. Instead, he blamed the system as a whole—starting with himself as CEO and including all the plant executives. True to his nature, he was thinking systemically. In response to this tragic event, Paul set up a series of rules and routines to enforce worker safety, including:

All accidents must be reported to Paul within twenty-four hours.

All accident reports must include an action plan to prevent similar accidents.

Failure to comply with the above was grounds for immediate dismissal. In addition, Paul raised the safety audit to the level of a financial audit and sought input on safety and improvement from frontline staff, who were encouraged to submit their ideas to managers. If managers did not listen or act, frontline workers were invited to call Paul any time, day or night. *He gave them his personal phone number*, and in doing so, opened

10 Ibid. p. 99. Kindle location 1577.

the doors to frank, honest, and open communication.

In contrast to Jack Welch, Paul O'Neil did not fixate on financial performance, market share, or any of the traditional measures of corporate performance. His focus was workplace safety. He wanted a zero-accident workplace—a towering objective in a manufacturing setting.

Like Jeff Kaas, Paul cared about people and their families, and he wanted workers to feel safe on the job. Consequently, he designed organizational DNA that made leaders focus on worker safety. He made safety the lens through which every system and process was measured. If there was a way to make a process safer, it was implemented. If an administrative system or process could be made safer, it was made safer. As a result, waste was eliminated and replaced with value. Quality shot up. Costs went down. Profits went up. Over the thirteen years Paul led the company, market valuation of Alcoa surged from $3 billion to $27.5 billion and net income rose from $200 million to $1.5 billion, while also making Alcoa one of the safest places to work in America. When Paul retired, it was safer to work in an Alcoa foundry with 2000° (F) liquid aluminum flowing around than in the back office of an insurance company shuffling paper.

Debrief

Paul O'Neil set safety as his primary focus and put Alcoa on a course toward something transcendent and more important than market share and profit: employee safety. With this system, Alcoa increased safety, but also created the best economic performance in its history.

Service, relationship, safety? These are all transcendent values. I don't remember anyone talking about transcendent values when I was earning my MBA, but they transcend generational values and character. My guess is that your undergraduate or graduate school training taught you workforce engagement is driven by a nice salary, a good benefits package, and a few recognition trinkets. Yet, all the research says no. What drives workforce engagement is the workers' relationship with their manager—a basic interaction among human beings. Are people treated with dignity, respect, service, and relationship? And, as in the case of an aluminum foundry, is their safety a top priority?

If you are a millennial just beginning your first management role and emerging as a potential leader, an important opportunity to consider lies here: What do you want your staff to experience from your leadership? Should it be one of production at any price? Do you only want to focus on getting the results needed to get bonuses?

My research tells me transcendent purpose, where people are valued above all else, creates the employee experience. Imagine a town with an Alcoa foundry on one side and a production-centered plant on the other. Who would choose to work for the production-centered plant, which, by nature, puts people in danger to maintain production targets? My guess is everyone would choose the foundry where safety is clearly a priority and every worker has the opportunity to contribute to making it even safer.

The leadership lesson is to capture the value of an engaged workforce by steering a transcendent course. Doing so will not undercut economic performance. It will drive it. Millennials are confident and smart enough to know when they are being treated well, and they will walk if they are not. Research clearly demonstrates that millennials have little organizational loyalty. Why should they? They believe they are special and can accomplish anything they set their minds to—we taught them that—so when they are not treated like they are special, they just find another job. Since 60 percent of millennials are looking for a different job at any given time, organizations clearly are not getting the message.

The next chapter tells the story of an iconic healthcare organization that changed its transcendent purpose from safety to revenue generation and the enrichment of surgeons. It was a costly mistake.

CHAPTER 4

AVOIDING A TOTAL SYSTEM FAILURE

"An organization's culture of purpose answers the critical questions of who it is and why it exists. They have a culture of purpose beyond making a profit."

— Punit Renjen, Deloitte CEO

Servant leadership, engagement, relationships, and safety all reflect transcendent values. They speak to something greater than profit or earnings per share. Yet, in the long-term, they accelerate and drive profit, growth, earnings, and performance. I have discovered that high-performing organizations do not just have a mission; they also have a purpose for their leadership that drives them toward their mission. This is the output or purpose of their system of leadership. A system's purpose can be likened to an iceberg where we only see the top 10 percent. Purpose is the 90 percent below the waterline. A system's purpose is like this. It might be unseen, yet it sets the organization's course and direction. Ignore this reality and an organization can easily find itself in the frigid waters of the North Atlantic abandoning ship.

*****

Nils August Johanson was twenty-one when he left his native Sweden for the shores of the USA. Like so many immigrants before and after him, he was looking to make his mark on the world in the land of opportunity. His ambition was to be a doctor. Ten years after arriving, he completed his medical training at the University of Denver and moved to Seattle, Washington. In 1908, he enlisted the support of ten local businessmen and founded the first modern nonprofit healthcare organization in Seattle. Out of respect for his homeland, it was called Swedish Medical Center—locals simply call it Swedish. As it grew, it became highly respected for exhibiting the highest ideals of a nonprofit healthcare institution. For more than a century, it built a reputation that focused on high quality patient care, compassion, safety, and community.

In 2011, Swedish was acquired by Providence Health & Services, making Providence one of the largest healthcare systems in the nation. Not long after, the Swedish Neuroscience Institute (SNI) was restructured to increase surgical volume and, therefore, revenue. By 2015, "It had the highest Medicare reimbursements per inpatient visit of any US hospital with at least 150 beds."[11] Five of the six highest revenue-generating surgeons in the State of Washington operated out of the Swedish Neuroscience Institute. It had become a money-making machine. Then disaster struck.

In 2017, *The Seattle Times* published a four-part exposé on the institute. As a result, the hospital CEO resigned and the institute's director lost his medical license due to high-risk, unethical medical practices and actual harm to patients. Federal regulators initiated an investigation that threatened to shut down SNI unless it addressed regulatory compliance issues. The exposé outlined critical systemic changes that resulted in significant short-term revenue growth, but lost the culture that put patient safety first.

Maybe dollar signs clouded management's judgment and the hospital only saw a financially thriving service, but the ethical ramifications led

11 Baker, Mike and Justin Mayo. "A Lost Voice, High Volume, Big Dollars, Rising Tensions, Double Book Surgeries." *Seattle Times*. Four-part exposé. February 10, 2017, May 28, 2017, August 10, 2017, and December 29, 2017.

to disciplinary actions and tarnished the reputation of an iconic non-profit institution.

When I interviewed Mike Baker, a co-author of the *Seattle Times* article, he said when Swedish initiated its restructuring, focus shifted from patient safety to revenue generation. An example of this shift was a surgeon incentive program. Each surgeon was financially rewarded based on the revenues they personally generated. This replaced an earlier model of revenue sharing that encouraged surgical collaboration. Financially, the change worked. The number of surgeries skyrocketed.

When Swedish changed the way surgeons were compensated, it re-engineered the DNA of its leadership—replacing a genetic code that had focused on patient safety for decades with a new code designed to make surgeons, already earning seven-figure salaries, even richer. Changing the purpose from patient safety to revenue generation was a seismic change.

As author and environmental scientist Donella Meadows says, "A change in [systems] purpose changes a system profoundly, even if every element and interconnection remain the same."[12] By changing the purpose of their system from patient safety to revenue generation, foundational rules, routines, and behaviors that created a culture of patient safety were exchanged for rules, routines, and behaviors that created revenue. Collaboration between doctors turned into competition. Team was turned into "me." Trust was replaced by distrust.

Systems are powerful. They can be designed with sequoia DNA—made to last and thrive through fires, drought, wind, and oppressive competition. Nils August Johanson set out to build a sequoia. But modern leaders, failing to understand the power of his system, turned

---

12 Meadows, Donella H. *Thinking in Systems: A Primer*. Chelsea Green Publishing. Kindle Edition, 2008. Kindle location 443.

lose a chainsaw on this iconic healthcare institution, scarring it for years to come.

Debrief

When I started this project, I was not expecting to confront transcendent leadership. The whole idea made me nervous. Yet in finding organizations that achieved elite levels of performance over long periods, transcendent leadership is exactly what I found. However, I found personal leadership is not transcendent; organizational systems are transcendent. Every individual leader was leading to the transcendent value determined by the organization. The US Army, Kaas Tailored, SCF healthcare, and Paul O'Neil at Alcoa Aluminum all built systems of leadership that focused on producing a singular transcendent value. They did not rely on individual leaders' goodwill.

A transcendent system's key indicator is whether everyone's voice is valued and respected. Kaas Tailored, SCF, and Alcoa Aluminum established leadership systems where every voice had the potential to innovate and/or transform the company.

What I found, is that high-performing organizations, those that produce long-term greatness, have systems that give every voice value. In designing your system and building your potential as a leader, think about how you hardwire this idea of "voice" into your leadership DNA. Making it a value is a nice idea, but it must be hardwired into the way you interact with staff and colleagues. It must be built into your organization's operational DNA or it is nothing but hot air rhetoric.

Section 3 will demonstrate how the highest-performing organizations hardwire transcendent values into their DNA through the genetics of rules, routines, and behaviors, and in doing so, build their employee experience, turning the workforce into ambassadors for the brand. In the next section, I will demonstrate how organizations develop key organizational resources to create maximum value and provide a path to innovation.

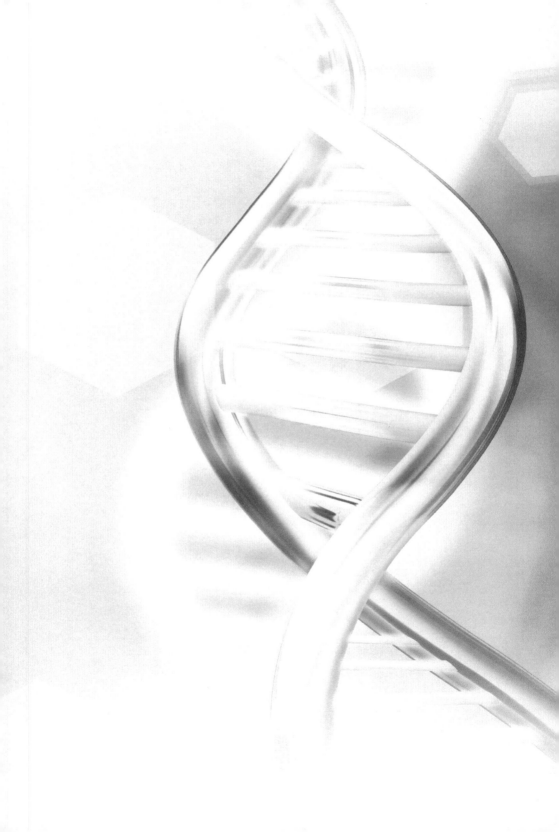

CHAPTER 5

LEADERSHIP DEBRIEF AND EXERCISES

"Give me a place to stand, and a lever long enough,
and I will move the world."

— Archimedes

A system's purpose is its most powerful aspect, and because of its sheer mass, it drives the system's behavior. Therefore, getting purpose right is critical. A leadership system may be the same as organizational purpose, but frequently, the two are different. An organizational leadership system's purpose is the outcome of leadership, and it is always closely tied to the workforce's experience. Intuitively, this makes sense. Wise leaders understand the worker's experience will be passed on to the customer.

You can do the following exercise yourself, with your team, or even with your family. But there is value in starting with yourself.

1. List three to five things your team needs from you. By limiting the list to three to five, you will be forced to think of the big picture. Look at it from the workers' perspective, not your own.

_____

_____

_____

_____

_____

2. From your list, pick one single idea. You may find yourself coming to something that borders on the transcendent. That should be expected because the transcendent is where all great systems start.

_____

_____

_____

_____

_____

_____

3. Look at yourself from your team's perspective. What do they get from you?

_____

_____

_____

_____

_____

_____

4. Now for the hard part—ask them what they need from you? If you are totally uncomfortable doing this, ask some peers.

_____

_____

_____

_____

_____

_____

5. Describe the link between your single idea and your organizational mission and/or vision.

_____

_____

_____

_____

_____

_____

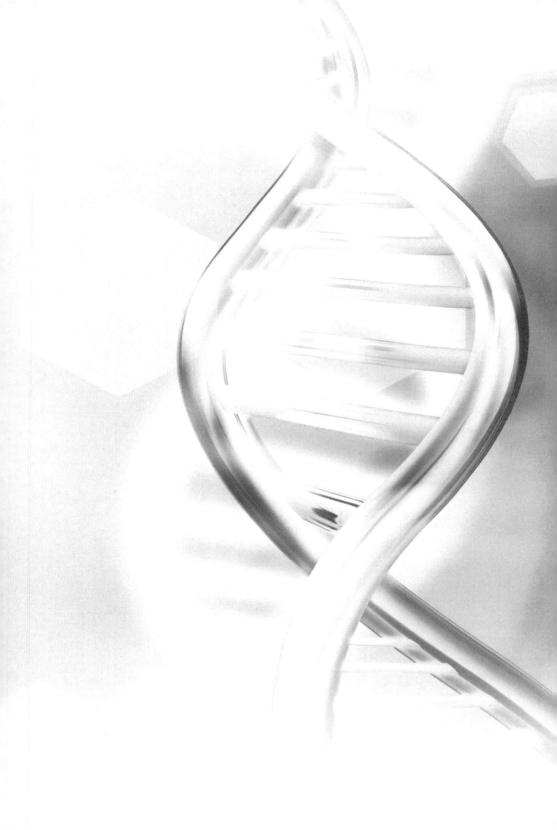

SECTION 2

BECOMING A DELIBERATELY DEVELOPMENTAL ORGANIZATION

"Effective leadership is about reliance on a well-constructed, continuously improving system that long outlives any leader, no matter how dynamic.... It's really about how the whole system holds together, and every single leader is committed to and expected to follow the standards."

— Sarah Patterson, Executive Director, Virginia Mason Institute

Every organization has three essential resources that turn ideas into valuable products and services: people, money in its broadest sense, and specialized knowledge. This section will demonstrate a fundamental shift in the way high-performing organizations understand these resources in contrast to how average organizations understand them. It is the difference between control and development.

***

In 1920, six physicians from the Mayo Clinic and the University of Virginia moved their families to Seattle, Washington, and founded the nonprofit Virginia Mason Hospital (VMH). Their goal was to approach medicine differently by creating a hospital where physician collaboration and teamwork would produce outstanding patient care. For nearly eighty years, growth was rapid, as VMH became a highly respected healthcare institution. The hospital eventually grew to 336 beds, opened multiple clinics throughout the Seattle metropolitan area, and employed 445 physicians. However, trouble was brewing. In 1998, VMH suffered its first financial loss, followed by another financial loss in 1999. By 2000, it was clear that Virginia Mason had to change, as did healthcare in general. A report by the Institute of Medicine said an estimated 98,000 Americans died each year from preventable causes in US hospitals.[13] This report ranked preventable hospital deaths among the leading causes of death in America. Healthcare was a bad value. It was too expensive and poor quality.

Virginia Mason was not immune from preventable deaths. In 2004, Mary McClinton, a much-loved grandmother, was being treated for a brain aneurysm. While being prepared for surgery, instead of being

---

13 Kenney, Charles. *Transforming Health Care*. Boca Raton, FL: CRC Press, 2010. p. 2.

injected with contrast dye for the procedure, she was injected with chlorhexidine, an antiseptic that cleans bacteria from skin prior to an incision. The accident stemmed from confusion over three identical stainless-steel bowls, all containing clear liquid, one of which was the antiseptic. Mrs. McClinton died within days. For the hospital, this tragedy was personal because the chief medical officer had been McClinton's personal physician for many years. Accidents like this were causing major insurance carriers to press for changes that would control costs. The twin pressures of low quality and high costs created a vortex that demanded change.

In 2001, Virginia Mason's executive team determined a radical new approach for reaching the twin goals of higher quality and lower costs. Unfortunately, no models in healthcare showed how to achieve these goals. Dr. Gary Kaplan and his executive team did something radical. They found a management model completely outside the healthcare industry, adopting the Toyota Production System (TPS).

TPS had turned a struggling truck manufacturer on the verge of bankruptcy in 1949 into the world's most profitable auto company. Toyota's production system is based on continually seeking perfection. Kaplan and his team decided if perfection was good enough for cars, it was even better for patients.

However, the idea was not without controversy. This radical and unprecedented step by the leadership of a financially troubled healthcare institution did not go unnoticed. When the entire executive team left for a ten-day junket to Japan to see how Toyota built cars, many of the employees were outraged. Nor was the irony lost on the community. On the evening before they left, a headline in the *Seattle Times* questioned the wisdom of a hospital paying for thirty executives to visit Japan so they could think "Lean."

However, what the executive team saw in Japan convinced them the Toyota Production System would turn Virginia Mason around. They became the first hospital in the world to adopt TPS, and today, they are the world's leader in applying Lean (the Americanized name for TPS) manufacturing principles to healthcare.

The results are staggering. As of 2020, Virginia Mason has received the following recognition:

- They have earned their seventeenth consecutive "A" in the Leapfrog Hospital Safety Grade Program, for success in preventing medical mistakes and other potential harm.
- They received the Distinguished Hospital Award for Clinical Excellence from Healthgrades eight consecutive years, placing Virginia Mason in the top 5 percent of the nearly 4,500 US hospitals.
- They received Healthgrades highest award for patient experience for eight consecutive years.
- They were recognized by *U.S. News and World Report* for eight consecutive years as one of the region's best hospitals.

Few healthcare organizations in the world can match Virginia Mason's performance record. The leadership became so good at applying Lean to healthcare that they spun off this expertise, forming the Virginia Mason Institute. This training organization now teaches other hospitals worldwide how to apply Lean to improve clinical outcomes, create the perfect patient experience, reduce or eliminate surgical and outpatient errors, improve workforce engagement, reduce turnover, and improve cash flow.

A central feature in Lean healthcare training is leadership's role in the cultural transformation required to maximize the value of Lean. By some estimates, 90 percent of all Lean initiatives fail to achieve any value. That means the other 10 percent generate enormous value. From my experience, the difference is leadership, or more precisely, the system of leadership. Virginia Mason has been so successful with Lean and the Toyota Production System because it has embraced both the tools of Lean and the system of leadership required to maximize Lean's value. The two are different and receive different titles. The Virginia Mason Production System (VMPS) uses Lean's tools and techniques. However, the Virginia Mason Management System (VMMS) is its system of leadership.

Traditionally, "buy in" from senior leaders was thought to be the key to successfully adopting Lean. This is not true. Many organizations adopt Lean as a one-off, occasional project to improve a process. It works, sort of. However, to fully recognize Lean's value, the organization must lose the archaic follower of the leader model of leadership, in favor of a leadership system designed with a unique DNA to engage the entire workforce. Virginia Mason calls this the Virginia Mason Management System (VMMS), which it defines as "a leadership system that provides focus, direction, alignment, and method of management for daily work."[14] The two do not work independently. As a practicing Lean practitioner, I have to confess, I have been very guilty of facilitating Lean workshops and events but never addressing the leadership system's role. To be honest, some have worked spectacularly well. However, more than I care to admit have failed because leadership was not prepared to empower its front-line staff to make decisions that would impact their own work and the value being delivered to customers.

---

14 Kenney, Charles. *A Leadership Journey in Health Care: Virginia Mason's Story.* Boca Raton, FL: CRC Press, 2015. p. 43.

Key Resources of the Leadership System

Every system has a set of key elements, or what I choose to call resources. These resources interact in specific ways to produce something of value—a purpose or outcome. The DNA molecule might be
the best illustration of this on the planet. The DNA molecule's basic
building blocks are sugar and phosphate, and within the phosphate,
a touch of oxygen—three elements found in most people's kitchens.
Yet their interaction forms the very foundation of biological life. This
understanding is one of the principle attributes of a system: It takes
one plus one and creates ten.

The three critical elements/resources every organization has are: 1)
people, 2) money, and 3) specialized knowledge/information. (I am
using the term money in the broadest sense. Technically, it also includes plant and equipment as well.) From my research and twenty-five years of consulting, the number one difference I see in average
versus high-performing organizations is: average organizations see
these resources as assets to be managed. Managed is a diplomatic way
of saying controlled. Organizations that consistently perform at elite
levels understand people, money, and knowledge and information, as
resources that can be developed.

Virginia Mason and the other organizations I researched are models
in their understanding that these resources can be developed to provide ever-increasing value to patients and customers. When I saw this
at Virginia Mason, I was stunned. Nothing in my entire career—consulting at hundreds of organizations and as a Baldrige Examiner (volunteer)—prepared me for what I saw. I was so surprised that I asked
Dr. Barbara Kellerman of Harvard's Kennedy School of Government
to help me digest it. She immediately understood what I had seen and
referred me to *An Everyone Culture* by Robert Kegan and Lisa Las-

kow Lahey, both of Harvard. In this book, the authors detail how three leading companies—Bridgewater Associates, The Decurion Corporation, and Next Jump, Inc.—create cultures that deliberately develop human capabilities. And these capabilities include both personal and professional skills. They call these companies DDOs (Deliberately Developmental Organizations).

Virginia Mason is a DDO. I have never seen an organization so intentional about developing its people. But I also saw how its leadership sees money and financial assets as resources that can also be developed. In their application of Lean, they are relentless about finding and removing waste. When they find it, they eliminate it, replacing waste with value for their patient-customers.

But they don't stop there. They are just as relentless about developing new knowledge and information. They have become a rabid learning organization where every time they learn something new, whether a surgical procedure or better patient release procedure, they immediately build the new knowledge into daily operations.

The great lesson here is that every leader and manager at Virginia Mason knows exactly what they are doing to develop their resources—people, money, knowledge/information. They have a game plan and they have integrated it into their system of leadership. Their system requires them to know how to develop these resources, and they are held accountable within the process. In the next three chapters, I will explain how Virginia Mason and others are creating new value, engaging the workforce, and building cultures where innovation is an everyday cultural habit.

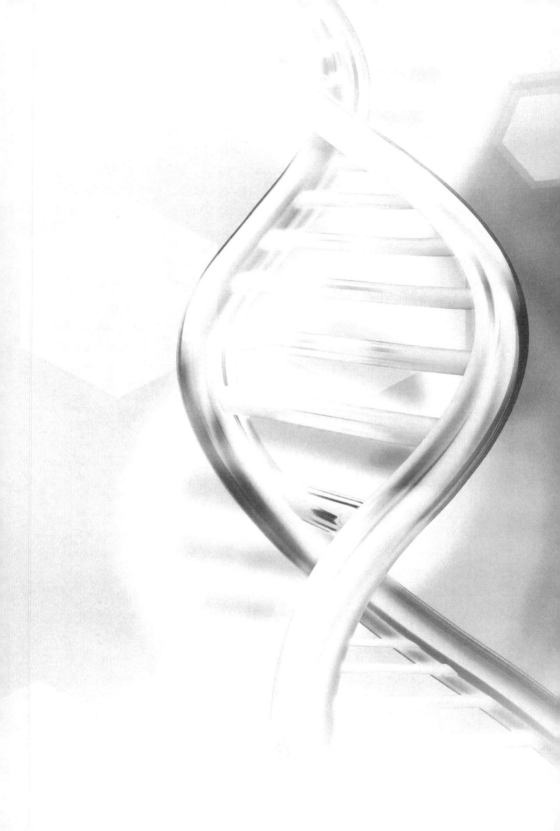

CHAPTER 6

DEVELOPING TOTAL HUMAN CAPACITY

"Leaders in a DDO have a deep conviction that our weaknesses
are pure gold if we will only dig into them."

— Robert Kegan and Lisa Laskow Lahey, *An Everyone Culture*

It is one of those moments tattooed into my brain. It's early morning. I am sitting across a table from an elementary school principal. Outside her office, 450 children are making their way to their classrooms. As she is talking to me about leadership, a subject she says she knows nothing about, she is explaining her approach for developing her teachers' skills. Her approach seems to emphasize developing her staff's total human capacity—not just the bits the district's budget paid for, but the entire breadth of human potential and opportunity. When I ask her if I am hearing this correctly, she looks at me with dismay and says, "Yes, why would I want half a teacher walking in the door?" The same could be said of a software engineer, a civil engineer, an accountant, a lawyer, a carpenter, or a US Army sergeant.

If you are an emerging leader, a seasoned executive, or a middle manager, you can look at your people in two ways: 1) corporate assets to be managed, directed, and controlled, or 2) resources of unlimited potential and opportunity with an innate capacity for creativity, problem solving, and innovation. Based on my research, the highest-performing organizations take the latter approach. Consequently, they reap the benefit of a workforce that is intellectually and psychologically engaged. These organizations produce more value, with less cost, and higher customer satisfaction. Why? Because they understand the most valuable bits of their workforce, this human capacity for creativity and innovation, come with the body they hire and at no additional cost. The job of leadership, then, is not to find it. It is already there. It walks in the door every morning, sits in the cubicle next to you, and eats lunch in the same lunchroom. The job of leadership is to design the leadership system so that fear and disrespect are eradicated in the workplace.

The challenge is to scale a system of leadership across the organization so every leader and manager knows exactly what they need to do to unleash this basic human capacity of creativity and innovation. Organizations that consistently perform at the highest levels do not rely on individual leaders' goodwill. They custom-engineer their leadership DNA so that every leader and manager becomes a miner looking for gold.

***

Recently, I gave a presentation on how leadership is an organizational system. Twenty senior leaders were in the conference room. First, I had them write down just one or two words to describe leadership's purpose or outcome. I received twenty-nine different responses. They were all good. Not a thing wrong with any of them. However, I am confident that if I were to ask twenty senior leaders at Virginia Mason Hospital to do the same, I would receive one response: respect. Respect for the work, respect for the worker, and respect for the patient or customer. Respect is what drives the entire institution. It is also what drives VMH's leaders to understand that a person, a worker, anyone who interfaces daily with the patient or customer, is a human being who walks through the door with unimaginable capacities. For

Virginia Mason, respect is not only a philosophical or moral statement of human value. Seeing people as a resource that can be developed means turning raw ore into pure gold that can drive the perfect patient experience, error-free healthcare, and daily medical innovation. It all begins with respect.

In one of their early trips to Japan leaders at Virginia Mason received an important lesson in respect and just how important it would need to be in their adoption of the Toyota Management System. They were visiting a Hitachi manufacturing plant, learning how to identify waste. They were split into two teams and told to work within bright white lines painted on the floor. However, they frequently strayed and were told by their sensei (teacher) that they could stand on one side of the line or the other, but they were not to stand on the line. As one of the VM leaders observed, "He was being kind of a pain in the butt about it." Finally, in exasperation, their sensei explained that the white lines were safety zones and they needed to be bright and clean. Furthermore, every night the supervisor (read this clearly, the *supervisor*) would clean these lines out of respect for the workers and their safety. Furthermore, they were told not to stand on the white lines, "out of honorable respect for the person who painted it."[15]

This concept of respect drives some rather unusual expectations for individual leaders. For example, leaders and managers are *not* allowed to solve problems for their staff. Doing so is disrespectful because solving a problem for a subordinate undermines the belief that human beings are highly intelligent and capable of solving complex problems. When a leader or manager solves a problem that a subordinate can solve, it robs the worker of an opportunity for personal and professional growth. While it might make the leader feel good, for the

---

15 Kenney, Charles. *A Leadership Journey in Health Care*: Virginia Mason's Story. Boca Raton, FL: CRC Press, 2015. p. 54.

worker, it reinforces the demeaning nonsensical belief that leaders are better human beings than followers. What an individual leader can do is help frame the problem. They can help their followers understand the problem's breadth and scope, but they are not to solve it. For those with natural leadership abilities, this idea of intentionally not being a problem solver borders on insanity. As Rhonda Stewart, Transformational Sensei at Virginia Mason Institute, told me, "Traditional leaders have a really hard time with this and many of them don't stick around very long." However, the story has another side: When leaders consistently push problem-solving down to those closest to the problem, two things happen: 1) front line staff become motivated to learn basic problem-solving skills, which is an increase in professional value, and 2) their confidence soars, which is an increase in personal self-confidence. As Rhonda related to me, "In this environment, we see staff with lots of ability but little confidence absolutely flourish." What Virginia Mason has discovered is that one simple rule, based on a purpose of respect, unleashes the basic human capacity for learning, growth, creativity, and innovation.

Respect also means they want to provide opportunities for staff to step out of their comfort zones and take a risk, yet do so in a safe place. Every Friday afternoon, in an auditorium that seats 125 people, Virginia Mason holds a weekly "report out." Members of a process improvement (Lean) team then provide a formal report on their results. All staff members are invited to the auditorium or to join via video streaming. During the meeting I attended, there were six report outs. Lean initiatives ranged from improving complex medical procedures to discharging patients with sepsis.

While the content of the reports was beyond me, I could easily observe the process—and it was exquisite. I felt like I was watching an artist at work. Each report was presented by two people and lasted exactly five minutes. I assumed team leaders were presenting. Not so. By design, presenters were rank and file members of the Lean team. Virginia Mason recognizes that public speaking is people's number one fear, so they encourage team members to take this opportunity to speak publicly. It engages the workforce in improving their medical skills *and* develops self-confidence. Even though public speaking can be terrifying, the auditorium feels like a safe place to practice (because it is).

The first words each presenter said were, "I would like to thank the members of my team and (the person standing next to them)." These simple words offer verbal recognition of each participant.

At the end of the hour, the chief medical officer stood to conduct a quick debrief. However, before he began, he acknowledged a woman sitting in the back of the auditorium. She had taken part in her first report out, and he recognized her by name for participating. Then at the very end, he again recognized her by name and thanked her for participating. I'm sure it was part of the design.

But just how far will Virginia Mason take this notion of respect? What happens when highly paid medical professionals with egos to match are asked to behave differently? These professionals drive the economic engine of modern hospitals, so many in healthcare are reluctant to offend them.

An interesting story tests Virginia Mason's core value of respect. One day, a nurse was prepping a cancer patient for chemotherapy. She noticed two required tests had not yet been completed and told her directing physician, who told her to proceed anyway. She had to choose between orders and doing what she thought was right for the patient. Respect dictated that the patient was her highest priority, so she called the chief of cancer services, who, in turn, called the physician to tell him the two tests must be done before delivering the chemotherapy.

Furious, the physician let loose on the nurse, verbally abusing her. She again called the chief of cancer services, who pulled a Patient Safety Alert (PSA), the equivalent of a Toyota worker pulling the stop cord, bringing production to a halt so an error does not get passed on. The chief of cancer services called the physician again, this time telling him his conduct was unprofessional, abusive, and in violation of Virginia Mason's value of respect. He was sidelined until a formal investigation could be completed. At Virginia Mason, respect is sacred, and it starts with their leadership system.

***

Kaas Tailored also takes the opportunity to seriously develop total human capacity. Jeff wants his staff to be experienced with *kaizen*. As noted earlier, *kaizen* is a Japanese word roughly meaning improvement. *Kaizen* is the basis for what Americans call Lean. By training his workforce in *kaizen* and rewarding them when they apply it, Jeff has developed a team with outstanding professional skills. He wants *kaizen* to be second nature for his staff, so he rewards them even if the *kaizen* is strictly personal. In an interview with one of Kaas Tailored's senior leaders, I heard stories of people receiving PTO (paid time off) for doing a *kaizen* on organizing a boat. On the lighter side of *kaizen*, Tucker Kaas, Jeff's son, decided to "help" his very pregnant wife by reorganizing her kitchen pantry. She was not pleased with the reorg. No blood was spilled, but the young husband learned a very important lesson. However, he had done a formal *kaizen*, so he received his PTO from Kaas Tailored. I guess it really is the thought that counts.

While Jeff knows that training his staff in daily *kaizen* develops professional skills, he also recognizes that practicing *kaizen* daily develops self-confidence in his staff, many of whom are recent immigrants.

While innumerable books have been written about helping leaders gain self-confidence, Jeff seems to take a different approach. He has developed a system in which mentors, supervisors, and production managers are trained in coaching and mentoring staff. This practice not only gives his coaches and mentors (leaders) self-confidence, but in the process, his workforce gains self-confidence because they are given the opportunity to contribute. Their voices are heard and respected. Practicing *kaizen* allows every member of the workforce to fully participate in the firm's success. If they see an opportunity to reduce waste by improving a process, they can fully participate in seeing their idea contribute to the company's success. With this system, every employee initiates, on average, five to six *kaizen*s each year. While not every employee participates, most do, and the result is that each *kaizen* saves the company about $1,000.

But Jeff pushes this idea of personal and professional development even further. Jeff does not separate personal and business values depending on economic expedience—actually, he doesn't separate them at all. As he explained, adopting *kaizen* from the Toyota production system came down to a really simple question: "Do I give a shit?"

Jeff looked deep to see if he truly cared for each team member, the whole person who walked through the door every day? Or did he just want to develop the bits he paid for? His personal mandate, and the mandate of his leadership system, is to practice servant leadership. This mandate has forced him to make some tough decisions.

As I mentioned, once trained and acclimated into Kaas Tailored's system, Jeff's workers become highly valued at other organizations. Jeff's employees represent an ethnic melting pot. Access to higher-paying jobs is critical to their families and their assimilation into American life. In keeping with his servant leadership values, Jeff expanded training so his employees could grow and become better able to move to these higher-paying jobs when they were available. When I asked how he might measure the results of his leadership system, he said, "I don't know, but I think it will eventually be the number of employees we can train and then move to another firm where there is more opportunity and they can better provide for their families."

Virginia Mason and Kaas Tailored are not the only organizations that deliberately develop both personal and professional attributes. Another exponentially larger organization has been developing people for years, and it is widely recognized as being the very best in the world at developing leaders—the US Military.

***

No institution in the world puts more emphasis on developing its workforce than the US Military. After my interview with General McCaffrey, I realized it is impossible to describe the difference between the Army and the average organization's approach to developing their workforce. It is a difference so wide it is impossible to calculate.

For example, when I was having lunch with Brian, the young millennial referenced in Chapter 2 who had recently been promoted to a leadership position with one of the world's largest engineering firms—a firm with 19,000 employees and $5 billion in revenue. When he told me about his promotion, I said, "Let me guess. When they gave you this promotion, they sent you off to leadership development school for a month so you would have some idea what you were supposed to do?"

His eyes got big, and he said, "No, they gave me nothing, nothing at all."

Unfortunately, that is the norm. Only a third of all first-time managers receive any training, coaching, or mentoring at all. Compare this with the Army (it is probably the same for the other branches of the military) where every rank has its own school. Not a simple lecture-based, eight-hour course or a series of online classes, but an entire school dedicated to successfully executing the requirements of each rank. When I asked General McCaffrey about this, he laughed and said, "Yeah, when I became a one-star general, I had to go to a nine-month school on how to be a one-star general. Same thing for the second and third stars." When he earned his fourth star? Another nine-month school. (I wondered who taught four-star generals how to be four-star generals.)

In explaining the significance of this emphasis on training and development, McCaffrey recounted an amazing story. During the first Gulf War (1990-1991), he commanded the 24th Infantry Mechanized Division. This command included nearly 26,000 soldiers, 1,600 armored vehicles, 3,000 wheeled vehicles, and 100 aircraft. His division executed the famed "left hook," where, in a bold and surprising move, his command and others hooked left across hundreds of miles of desert to surround and destroy the Iraqi army within forty-eight hours.

Left hook was a maneuver that many thought too risky because of its complexity. Three weeks before the kickoff, McCaffrey's chief of staff, his most important assistant, was promoted and reassigned. McCaffrey told me he asked the General of the Army (for us non-military types, the General of the Army is CEO to 1.3 million active duty and 0.7 million reserve personnel) if he could keep this officer for just another few weeks, until the maneuver was complete.

The response was, "No, he earned this promotion, and he will be reassigned to a command consistent with his new rank, one-star general."

A week later, the new chief of staff arrived and had two weeks to prepare troops for one of the most complex maneuvers in recent military history. As McCaffrey said, "He performed flawlessly, with no loss in performance." The general had no idea who the guy was; there was no time for on-the-job training, no time for assimilation into a unique culture; he had to show up and immediately perform. This situation only worked because the US Army knows the requirements of each rank and trains soldiers and officers relentlessly on how to succeed at each rank.

Observations

I love the sentiment expressed by Brené Brown in her book *Dare to Lead*: "I define a leader as anyone who takes responsibility for finding the potential in people and processes and who has the courage to develop that potential."[16] The challenge is to scale this sentiment so that every leader in your organization is leading to this end. In short, moving beyond the goodwill of individual leaders to make developing people systemic. Contrary to popular opinion, organizations are not a simple aggregation of individuals, but "systems of interacting elements: Roles, responsibilities, and relationships."[17] For many organizations, training and development are divorced from these critical organizational systems. The opportunity is to integrate development with a designed system that makes both the system and the individual successful.

Rob McKenna, PhD is the Chair of Industrial-Organizational Psychology Department at Seattle Pacific University. He is also the founder of

---

16 Brown, Brené. *Dare to Lead*. New York, NY: Random House. Kindle Edition, 2018. p. 10.
17 Beer, Michael et al. "Why Leadership Training Fails—and What to Do About It." *Harvard Business Review*. (October 2016) p. 6.

a training organization whose mission is WHOLE – INTENTIONAL- LEADER DEVELOPMENT or Wild Leadership. In a conversation with Rob and his partner, Daniel Hallack, PhD, regarding the integration of leadership development and organizational systems, they stated: "The integration and alignment of the individual leader within their organizational context is the key. That is when the prospect of developing whole leaders gets really interesting…learning is directly related to the needs of the organization around them."

My goal is not to prescribe specific ways to develop your workforce. My goal is to challenge the emerging leader or seasoned executive's thinking. Virginia Mason Hospital develops its workforce in ways appropriate to its unique organization, but it all starts with a purpose of respect. Respect is what drives the methods used to develop its people. It would be disrespectful to focus exclusively on professional development. Respect says VMH has to develop the whole person.

Servant leadership and giving an engaged workforce a purpose in finding and eliminating waste drives Kaas Tailored in developing their workforce. Because of their singular goal of engaging their workforce, they have dropped traditional titles. Mentors have replaced supervisors, managers, and directors. Every leader is trained in how to mentor and coach their staff on finding and eliminating waste. This mentoring mindset may sound like a change in semantics, but it drives the essential relationships between the staff.

In a similar way, the US Army, and each branch of the military, has identified specific methods to develop their workforce based on servant leadership principles. During my interview with Colonel Marc Gauthier, thirty-four-year Army veteran, Army Ranger, and member of the Special Forces, he explained that part of his regular routine was to meet with each of his officers four times a year. In these meetings, they reviewed performance, but primarily, these meeting were to coach officers on how to become better able to execute servant leadership's requirements. In this way, the Army is developing better officers, and the officers are reaping the benefits the Army offers. Perhaps it is just something he did individually, but my impression is it is part of the model.

All of the organizations we have looked at have designed their own methods of developing their workforces' full capacities. They have made the leap from relying on individual leaders' goodwill to making development systemic and integrated to the way they do leadership. This also includes the way they do leadership development. It is hard for an outsider to walk into a leadership position at Virginia Mason. They have to unload a lot of institutional baggage and think about leadership in a different way. I think the same is true at Kaas Tailored, and obviously, in the US Army.

A growing body of evidence indicates leadership training divorced from unique organizational systems of interlocking rules, routines, and behaviors offers little, if any, return on investment. In their article "Why Leadership Training Fails—and What to Do About It," published in the *Harvard Business Review*, Michael Beer and his colleagues tell the story of a company that invested heavily in team building and collaboration among the workforce:

> They [the company] found it impossible to apply what they had learned about teamwork and collaboration because of a number of managerial and organizational barriers: a lack of strategic clarity, the previous GM's top-down style, a politically charged environment, and cross-functional conflict.[18]

---

18 Beer, Michael et al. "Why Leadership Training Fails—and What to Do About It." *Harvard Business Review*. (October 2016) p. 6.

Even the sacred halls of Harvard University, which claims to educate leaders to "change the world," is coming under criticism. Duff McDonald, in his book *The Golden Passport*, says regarding this claim, "most of it is bullshit."[19]

In his book *Leadership BS: Fixing Workplaces and Careers One Truth at a Time*, Stanford University Professor Jeffrey Pfeffer says, "It is not just that all the efforts to develop better leaders...have failed to make things appreciably better.... It makes things much worse."[20]

When I spoke to a young worker about how his company does employee reviews, he explained that they don't do traditional annual reviews; it is more that they have conversations throughout the year. As he explained the process, it became clear these conversations were as much about personal as professional development. I asked, "What is the ratio between personal and professional emphasis?"

He replied, "About a 90 to 10 percent split."

I asked, "You mean 90 percent professional and 10 percent personal?"

He looked at me like I was from another planet.

"No, 90 percent is personal."

What would I do if I were just entering the workforce? I would look for the organization that best articulated how it would grow and develop my value. I would be specifically asking how it was going to make me a better human and fully integrate my work with my personal values.

---

19 McDonald, Duff. *The Golden Passport: Harvard Business School, the Limits of Capitalism, and the Moral Failure of the MBA Elite.* New York, NY: Harper Business, 2017. p. 314.
20 Pfeffer, Jeffrey. *Leadership BS: Fixing Workplaces and Careers One Truth at a Time.* New York, NY: Harper Collins, 2015. p. 5.

While the traditional answer is a generous employee tuition program, that usually ties you to the organization. These programs seldom produce a better employee or better human being. If the human resources professional interviewing me cannot explain specifically how they are going to coach, mentor, and grow my value, I would not walk out the door—I would run like my life depended on it. If you are reading these words while looking for a new job, be prepared to run a lot because while a few organizations understand the value of development, most don't have a clue how to do it, nor do they want to.

However, if you find one of these rare organizations, take whatever they offer because, in a few years, the world will be camping at your doorstep.

Leadership Debrief and Exercises

I am irritated by our current approach to leadership in general, but one of the most maddening aspects is the narcissistic notion of courageous leadership. Leadership gurus drone on about it, but they are speaking about personal leadership. This is a message from one person to another person. The great opportunity today is to create a workforce that is courageous. To scale these attributes requires a system. When we do this, we will launch a tidal wave of innovation and customer value.

Once again, put yourself at the center. Write down five to ten ways you intentionally develop your team, whether it's your management team, organization, or family. Write one idea per card or Post-it note.

1. Take your cards or Post-it notes and split them into two groups:

   A. Professional development

_____

_____

_____

B. Personal development

_____

_____

_____

_____

2. If you worked for yourself, would you be satisfied with the oppor-
    tunities for professional and personal growth and development? If
    not, why not; if so, why?

_____

_____

_____

_____

3. Ask your team what is more important to them: professional or
    personal development. Are they more interested in learning about
    how to grow in the organization or how to become a more whole
    person? More confident? More mission oriented? Do they want
    to learn more about maximizing personal goals or maximizing
    corporate goals?

_____

_____

_____

_____

4. Try to reconcile the differences between what you think is most
    important and what your team thinks is most important.

_____

_____

_____

_____

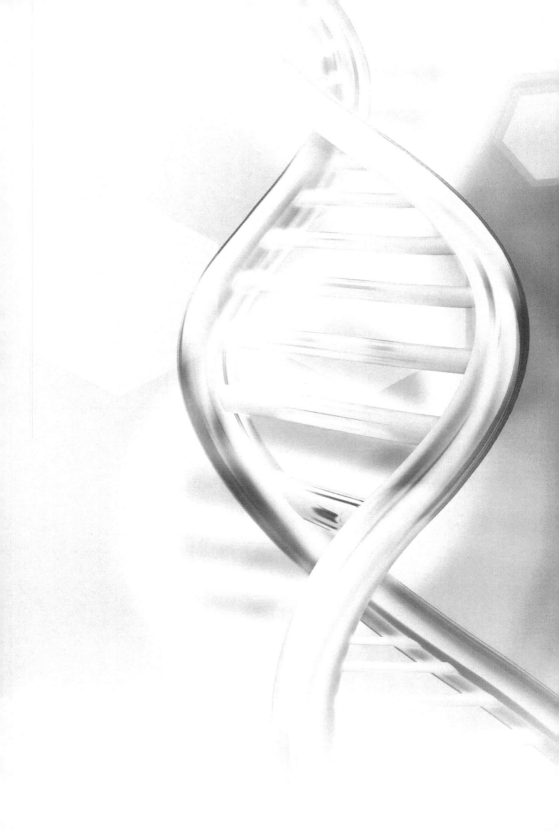

CHAPTER 7

DEVELOPING FINANCIAL VALUE

"Healthcare is close to a $3 trillion industry, that is over
17 percent of GDP. Many estimates are that somewhere
between 30 and 50 percent of it represents waste."

— Dr. Gary Kaplan, CEO Virginia Mason Medical Center

One thing that surprised me while conducting research into DDOs
(Deliberately Developmental Organizations) was their unique way of
looking at money. The best word I can use to describe their perspective
is value. Most of my twenty-five-year consulting career has been in the
public sector. For organizations in the public sector, money is budget,
and as long as the leader stays within the budget, they are doing a good
job. However, the DDOs I identified have a different definition of value
that goes beyond the dollars to everything dollars can buy—including
people, skills, technology, equipment, facilities, and services. That definition is one reason they embrace developing the whole person. They
see value in building the self-confidence of their staff, and the result is
both better employees and more money. They seem to abhor waste of
any kind and uplift all organizational resources as valuable.

***

At the World Economic Forum in January 2020, Chairman and Co-
CEO of Salesforce Marc Benioff declared, "Capitalism as we have

known it is dead." In his statement, he was not arguing capitalism versus socialism. He was arguing that traditional *share*holder-focused capitalism was dead, and *stake*holder capitalism was the voice of the future. This new era will require new models of leadership and a revolutionary new way of thinking about value.

For example, tomorrow, if a manufacturer meets its production targets and offers both low cost and high quality, but ignores safety concerns and someone is killed in the process, will customers believe they got maximum value? Something tells me the answer is no.

High-performing organizations create cultures where value rules. In this chapter, we will learn how high-performing organizations design leadership systems (the way leaders will lead) and train staff to grow cultures where creating value is a daily event and increases over time— not only for customers, but for the workforce and stakeholders as well.

***

As the Great Recession of 2008 began to roll through our worldwide economy, organizations of all kinds began successive rounds of layoffs. Peak global unemployment hit 10 percent, but in the US, many counties saw unemployment as high as 25 percent. The devastation came as close to the Great Depression as possible. If not for the billions of dollars the government infused into the economy, it would have been equal. Few institutions were spared. We all watched in dismay as major financial institutions collapsed. Lehman Brothers, America's fourth largest bank, collapsed virtually overnight. Other banking institutions such as Merrill Lynch, AIG, Freddie Mac, Fannie Mae, HBOS, and the Royal Bank of Scotland all needed government aid.

But the real devastation was more personal. Families everywhere saw their homes foreclosed upon, retirement savings wiped out, long-standing family businesses closed or went into bankruptcy. Newly constructed homes were abandoned by home buyers and sat vacant while cities tried to figure out who owned them so they could enforce city codes and bill for basic utilities.

Healthcare institutions were not immune to the economic devastation. Hospitals in Seattle, Washington, like many across the nation, were forced to lay off nurses and medical assistants to balance budgets.

Except one.

Virginia Mason Medical Center. They didn't lay off anyone. Furthermore, they continued to pay bonuses throughout the recession.

How was this possible?

Virginia Mason avoided laying off anyone because of its relentless pursuit of the perfect patient experience and error-free healthcare delivery. Just like Paul O'Neil created a lens of safety through which every process was measured, at Virginia Mason, every process and procedure was measured, monitored, and improved through the lens of respect: respect for the work, respect for the worker, and respect for the patient.

This process naturally finds and eliminates waste. It puts more value-added resources in front of the patient or customer. For example, when Virginia Mason began its Lean journey, nurses spent only 35 percent of their time with patients. The other 65 percent was spent doing low value work. Today, they spend more than 90 percent of their time with patients—high value work relative to the patient experience. But something else happens when 90 percent of a nurse's day is spent with patients as opposed to 35 percent.

They have more fun!

Nurses go to nursing school because they are passionate about helping people through pain and illness. On the afternoon I observed the weekly report out at Virginia Mason, I did not hear one word about money or productivity. All the reports were about improving safety, making life easier for patients, improving clinical outcomes, and providing error-free healthcare.

What happens when patient safety and satisfaction go up, clinical outcomes improve, and medical errors go down? Healthcare costs go down. Healthcare consumes nearly 17 percent of US GDP, with clinical outcomes no better than in other countries where healthcare is a fraction of the cost. Therefore, healthcare is of low value relative to its cost.

Healthcare organizations like Virginia Mason are working to make healthcare high quality and low cost. The key to lower cost and higher quality at Virginia Mason is a system of leadership where all leaders understand their part in finding and eliminating waste. At Virginia Mason, all leaders are part of the orchestra. Virginia Mason does not have hot-shot conductors. Their success has nothing to do with inspiring or charismatic leadership, not even the personal charm of Dr. Gary Kaplan, the CEO, or the general goodwill of the managers. At Virginia Mason, all leaders are trained into a system designed to eliminate waste and create error-free healthcare.

This understanding of value also extends to their facilities. Need to find the executive offices? Do not look up to the highest floor. Look down because they are in the basement. For many, an executive office with a beautiful view overlooking the city is a perk—a symbol of power and position. However, the space, relative to the mission of healing and a culture of respect, is of low value. Therefore, the executives' offices are in the basement, where the majestic views of Mt. Rainier and

Puget Sound are a distraction from healthcare's mission.

Expansive views of the Seattle waterfront and snowcapped mountains are reserved for patients. Putting executive offices in the basement is not a moral statement. It is part of an economic model and system of leadership that says leaders do their best work when they are not in their offices. In the next section, we will explore how Virginia Mason does not have an "open door" policy. Based on the purpose of respect, leaders are expected to go to their staff, rather than expecting staff to come to them. If a leader needs an "open door" policy, they are not doing their job correctly.

The result is some of the strongest financials in the industry. Virginia Mason simply creates more value for its patients, its workforce, and its community with fewer financial resources.

The afternoon I observed their weekly report outs, I witnessed an exquisitely designed process. Not a second was wasted. Reports on every Lean event were scripted to communicate with transparency, candor, and respect. Some Lean events seemed wildly successful. Others less so. That is how improvement happens. It can be three steps forward and two steps back, but progress is continually forward. But I saw something even more remarkable—a celebration of people, no matter their place in the hierarchy, and how they can drive organizational improvement. When the workforce is respected, valued, and celebrated, something happens to the economics. Simply stated, costs go down.

In the 2017 report "State of the American Workplace," Gallup provides a number that should capture the imagination of every CEO. Companies with the highest levels of workforce engagement enjoy profits 21 percent higher than those with the lowest.[21] The question is: Is anybody listening?

21 "State of the American Workplace." Gallup, 2017. p. 68.

As a Lean practitioner, I have seen too many teams struggle due to lack of support—buy-in from leadership. Leaders were dutiful in following the Lean process, but all the while, they were communicating their disrespect for the process, their staff, and their customers. This does not happen at Virginia Mason. All their leaders have to be certified in Lean and personally conduct one to three Lean events each year—including the CEO.

***

Jeff, at Kaas Tailored, takes a similar but different approach to Lean/*kaizen*. While both Virginia Mason and Kaas Tailored have adopted the system, we cannot assume their success is based on Lean only. The methodology works, but to maximize its potential, it must be integrated into a complimentary leadership system. Virginia Mason formalized its system, calling it the Virginia Mason Management System (VMMS). Kaas Tailored has a clearly defined system of leadership, but it has not been given a formal title. In both cases, a complimentary leadership system allows them to achieve outstanding economic performance. They come at it from approaches unique to themselves. Virginia Mason starts with respect. Kaas Tailored starts with servant leadership and engagement. It could be argued that they both end up at the same place. The point is that they each have a starting line, a purpose for their leadership that drives the way they eliminate waste and create value. The idea of servant leadership drove Jeff Kaas to eliminate his office, and respect drove Virginia Mason to put its executive offices in the basement.

This relentless pursuit of value is what allows Kaas Tailored to stay in business. Kaas is located in a region where companies like Boeing, Microsoft, Amazon, Google, and Apple all have major operations. Consequently, Kaas operates in an area with some of the highest wages and home values in the nation. By all standards, it should not be able to survive where it is. Yet it is able to compete against firms that operate in parts of the country, and even the world, with substantially lower labor costs. In the same way, this pursuit of eliminating waste allowed Virginia Mason to work through one of the most devastating recessions since the 1930s without a layoff.

What would happen if US manufacturing operated like Kaas Tailored and more hospitals operated like Virginia Mason? I think we would see a flood of high-quality manufacturing jobs coming back into the US. In addition, while there are certainly systemic reasons healthcare costs in the US are high relative to other nations, clearly, opportunity exists both to improve quality and reduce operating costs.

***

There are other ways, however, to think about developing financial resources. It is not always about eliminating waste and replacing it with customer value. At its core, developing financial resources is about maximizing *all* available resources for the customer's benefit. Though I will introduce her fully in the next section, I want to briefly mention an elementary school principal named Erin who took a failing school and helped it become one of the highest-performing schools in her district of 25,000 students within five years. Then her school turned it up another notch by becoming the only school to close the achievement gap for the next two consecutive years. Closing the achievement gap means closing the gaps in academic performance between majority and minority population groups or between rich and poor. It is a massive accomplishment.

Erin told me a story. At the end of her first year as principal, she received a budget report. She had a $14,000 surplus. Running a budget deficit is one of the quickest ways for a principal to get fired, so she was relieved. However, upon further review, she realized her surplus was because the church that used the school on Sundays had made a $15,000 donation. She had overspent her budget by $1,000.

Then Erin realized the little church represented a resource that could bring value to her students. She also realized other community groups could be tapped for the benefit of her students and their families. She embraced community groups, developing relationships with many of them. Today, the school is a community gathering place. It is a place where, once a month, families gather for movie night. Before school starts in the fall, community members spend a day volunteering to prepare classrooms, disinfect and clean equipment for medically fragile students, and pressure-wash playgrounds. Teachers also receive value from these relationships. When they have special in-service training and could use meals, community groups gladly step in to provide them, free of charge.

The result: Attendance at parent-teacher conferences has soared. Where parents and grandparents were once hesitant to attend school events because of their own lack of education, now they see the school as a place of safety and support. By tapping into these community groups, Erin brought additional resources into her classrooms, and at no additional cost to the district.

Community involvement is one of the key ingredients of schools that consistently close the achievement gap. They get the entire community focused on students' academic achievement. In a policy brief, the National Educational Association said, "Parent, family, and community involvement in education correlates with higher academic performance and school improvement."[22]

In my consulting career, I have worked with a lot of public sector leaders, including educators. Money is always an issue, and competition for it is fierce. Erin took a different route. Instead of fighting her district for more resources, she tapped into the free resources sitting on her doorstep. The result: More educational value delivered to her students and a student body with some of the highest levels of academic achievement in the district.

Observations

My goal is to challenge every emerging or seasoned executive's thinking. Maximizing the value of tools like Lean/*kaizen* requires a complimentary leadership and management system. Although I absolutely believe in the value of Lean, I am not trying to sell it. There are other tools that will improve operational processes. What I am selling is the idea that each of them requires a designed system of leadership to maximize its value and opportunities. In addition, financial value is sometimes not about eliminating waste. As we saw with Erin, it is about maximizing all the resources available that add value to the customer, which in her case, is the student. But this, too, requires an understanding of leadership that goes beyond power, control, management, and command. As we will see, Erin designed a system of leadership that produced collaboration among her faculty. Collaborating with existing community groups is just a natural extension of her system.

---

22 Policy Brief. "Parent, Family, Community Involvement in Education." 2008. p. 2.

Leadership Debrief and Exercises

You can do this exercise by yourself or with your team. However, it is good to start on your own. Here are some questions for reflection. Once you have developed your responses, then ask your team the same questions.

1. Whether you work in the for-profit or nonprofit world, your job and mine is to maximize value delivered to our customers. What is your value proposition? How do you define or understand the value you deliver to your immediate customer? Does every leader in your organization understand what this means, and more importantly, how do they and their teams contribute to it?

    _____

    _____

    _____

    _____

2. What detracts from the value your customers might receive? Obviously, operational waste is the major detractor, so what is your specific methodology for eliminating waste from your operations?

    _____

    _____

    _____

    _____

3. How do you calculate the financial returns on your method of eliminating waste from your operations?

_____

_____

_____

_____

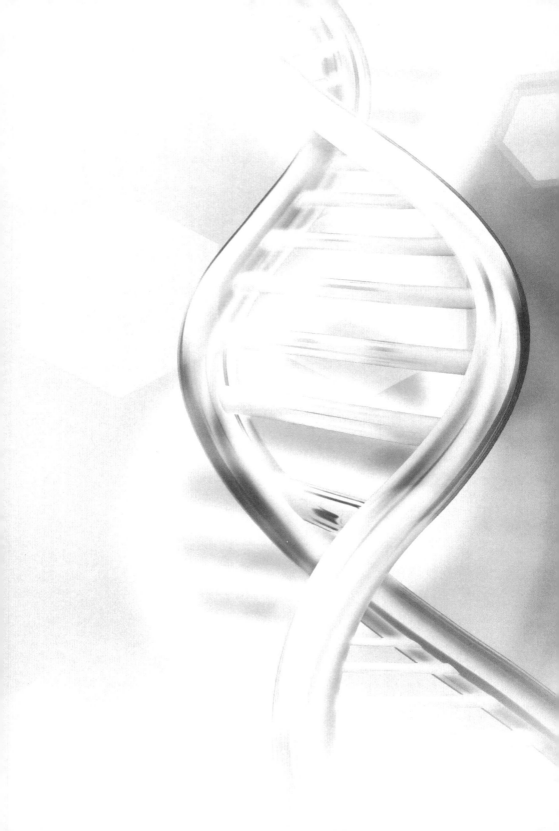

CHAPTER 8

DEVELOPING A CULTURE OF DAILY INNOVATION

"A manager is responsible for the application
and performance of knowledge."

— Peter Drucker

Think about your team or organization. How would you feel if you were so good at what you did that people lined up to see how you do it? Your customers are lining up. People and organizations you have never heard of are calling for your help. In the highest form of flattery, even your competitors are asking for your help (although they may be asking through a third party). In the six years prior to my tour of Kaas Tailored and my interview with Jeff Kaas, 40,000 people had visited the company's facilities. It's probably pushing 50,000 by now.

One day when I was reviewing my research and sketching out this manuscript, I was struck by the unexpected. Three of the organizations I am using as case studies are so good at what they do that they have been forced to spin off training and consulting organizations. Kaas Tailored is one of them. Its consulting organization is Truth Bit Bull Consulting, and its first two clients were a national retail clothing brand (a customer) and a major European nation's healthcare system.

Virginia Mason set up the Virginia Mason Institute (VMI). It is so good at implementing the Toyota Production System in healthcare that Toyota sends its healthcare leadership to VMI. VMI also contracts with hospitals worldwide that want to implement Lean.

Southcentral Foundation has become so good at delivering healthcare to indigenous people that it now trains and consults with healthcare organizations worldwide on its Nuka System of Care. Southcentral is so good that, in an interview with Anchorage's KTUU television, Dr. Berwick (administrator of CMS—Medicaid Services—under the Obama Administration) described the Nuka system of care as a "massive" departure from traditional healthcare models. He said, "Costs are too high, quality too low, but the Nuka system of care reverses this. They have some of the highest quality at highly sustainable costs."[23]

Yet each of these organizations has a learner mentality. When I told Jeff Kaas the subject of my research was about organizational systems of leadership, he said, "Oh, I want to know how to do that," even though he was clearly doing it already. Each of these organizations, and not just their individual leaders, has the collective notion that there is always something to learn and they wonder how they can improve their operations. Neither do they rely on the moment of light-bulb genius—they create cultures of everyday innovation. Every day seems to be a new opportunity to learn, and therefore, an opportunity to innovate.

***

Right now, someone is having an idea; it could be the next big breakthrough in cancer treatment, a revolutionary communications technology, or a sensor that will reduce auto accidents by 50 percent. Four million teachers would be thrilled to provide an idea to help a fourth grader read better. Twenty million healthcare workers have ideas about how to treat patients faster and cheaper. And fourteen million

23 https://www.youtube.com/watch?v=gg0qUCx9A68. Accessed May 21, 2020.

manufacturing workers see an opportunity to make an industrial process safer, cheaper, and faster. If you are a team leader or manage multiple teams, or you are a seasoned executive struggling with innovation, the solution is sitting right in front of you. It is not finding the next "big thing" but unleashing the creative juices of every member of your workforce. Your workers are more than willing to help, if you will only say "please." While I may be guilty of oversimplifying workforce engagement, the organizations in my research seem to experience innovation as the outcome of offering a safe place to work. By safety, I mean both physical and psychological safety. I think you will agree the math works better when 70 percent of the workforce is actively engaged instead of relying on the genius of one or two super-smart people.

Of the three key resources that every organization possesses, knowledge/information is the least appreciated and understood. For some reason, every organization believes it has the smartest people on the planet. The reality is very few organizations have an absolute lock on the best talent. However, organizations that consistently perform at a high level have found ways to unleash their entire workforce's creative juices. This means they are creating new knowledge and innovating new products every day of the week. They do not rely on the chief innovation officer's brilliance—his or her very existence announces to all that the workforce is incapable of innovation. One key attribute of a system is that the system will generate its own behavior, sometimes despite intentions to the contrary. Organizations and leaders who understand this design their leadership system to trigger the human capacity for creativity, ingenuity, and innovation. But it takes a specific kind of leadership—leadership that pushes power down the hierarchal ladder.

***

In 1982, when the US Federal Government turned over the health-care of 200 Native American tribes to Southcentral Foundation (SCF), SCF was hardly an experienced and fully integrated healthcare provider. It was small and inexperienced. Overnight, it had to set up financial and patient information systems, design practice areas, hire staff, and organize clinics. Nationally, access to basic healthcare for Native Americans is substantially less than that of the general population. Cancer mortality rates for Native Americans are among the highest of all racial and ethnic groups in the US. The Federal Indian Health Service (FIHS) reports that Native Americans' life expectancy is five-and-a-half years less than that of the average American, and they experience higher incidences of disease than the general population. FIHS also reports that Native Americans healthcare experiences are handicapped by inadequate education, poverty, discrimination in the delivery of care, and cultural differences.[24]

SCF is reversing this trend by challenging traditional Western medicine but not at the expense of clinical outcomes. Clinical outcomes in SCF rank in the nation's top 25 percent. Furthermore, they are producing these outcomes at lower cost than many of their contemporaries.

On the surface, SCF may look like any other healthcare system. It has a hospital and network of clinics strategically located to serve its patients. However, go below the service and you will see it has some radically innovative approaches that create a culture of innovation: 1) It does not refer to its patients as patients, but customer-owners. Patients is too passive; customer-owners communicates that the tribes own the system, which reverses decades of assimilation where self-determination was taken from them. 2) Where Western medicine ignores spirituality, if not outright scorns it, SCF celebrates it. 3) Where West-

24 Indian Health Service. "Indian Health Disparities."

ern medicine fixes a child's broken arm, SCF wants to fix the cause of the broken arm. 4) Where Western medicine focuses on the health of an individual patient, SCF wants to see healthy communities. As Dr. Donald Berwick, administrator of CMS during the Obama Administration, said, "SCF wants to see an empty hospital."[25] When hospitals are empty, the community is healthy. In contrast, Western medicine requires hospitals to be full because financial sustainability is their primary objective—necessary, yes; paramount, no.

However, there is more to SCF's DNA. They understand the value and role of storytelling. Until the development of a written form of Cherokee in the early 1800s, Native Americans relied exclusively on oral histories, preserving their history and culture through oral traditions. They recognize that everyone has a story and their individual story is coiled around stories that form a double helix, including family and community cultural genetics. While practitioners of Western medicine might want to learn a patient's medical history, their personal story is often ignored and seen as irrelevant to medical science.

SCF realizes medical history is completely interwoven with personal story, so they set up a healthcare system that focuses on relationships and respects the role and value of stories because they form the DNA of relationships. Maybe the kid's arm was broken because they were just playing hard, or maybe it was broken because of alcohol-related violence in the home; their parent may need emotional and psychological counseling because alcoholism runs through generations of the family. By providing social services in conjunction with medical services, SCF not only treats the broken arm but generates community health as well.

Relationships and stories drive how leaders lead and create a culture

25 Indian Health Service. "Indian Health Disparities."

where innovation is embraced and encouraged. Nuka, which, as mentioned before, is an Alaskan Native word meaning giant structures and living things, was not the result of years of academic theory, or think tanks evaluating reams of healthcare data. Nor was it the brilliant idea of CEO Katherine Gottlieb. It came about by understanding that the customer-owner was "royalty," and that they needed to design a system of care, including leadership, that met the needs of their entire network of 200 Native American tribes.

This system includes professional development plans (PDP) for every leader and worker. While PDPs are often seen as a disciplinary action or "opportunity for learning," at Southcentral Foundation, PDPs are empowering, and they knit daily work with strategy, innovation, continuous improvement, and added value for customer-owners. Therefore, every leader understands that PDPs are central to innovation for themselves and their staff. Innovation is not left up to a suggestion box in the staff lunchroom. It is built into the DNA of daily work and aligns with the organization's larger strategic objectives.

***

While SCF's approach to innovation is directly aligned to Native American values, Virginia Mason (VM) takes a more structured approach. When VM hires a leader from the outside, it provides a specific set of expectations designed for the new hire. One expectation is that the hire will be certified in Lean. This is an internal certification, and once certified, every leader is expected to personally conduct one to three Lean events a year. As a result, every leader becomes personally attached to Lean as a methodology for generating lower cost and daily innovation. It also means they are undertaking a lot of Lean events. My own unsubstantiated estimate is that the entire workforce, all 9500 of them, are participating in some kind of Lean or daily kaizen every day. That is a lot of mental horsepower focusing on a healthcare system already considered one of the nation's best.

***

SCF takes one approach to innovation, Virginia Mason another, and Kaas Tailored a third. Kaas Tailored favors the word *kaizen* over Lean, and it does Lean/*kaizen* differently. While Virginia Mason conducts Lean events, Kaas Tailored practices everyday *kaizen*. Anyone with a good idea can conduct their own *kaizen*. This requires a specific kind of leadership.

Leaders must be active mentors and coaches. Mentoring and coaching is not just a good idea—it is a requirement of Kaas Tailored's leadership system. The result is Kaas Tailored's 200 employees generate 1,000 to 1,250 *kaizen*s each year, and each one saves the company about $1,000. That is a lot of innovation going on, and it creates a culture of everyday innovation. Jeff Kaas is not waiting for the "next big thing"; he is creating little "big things" every day of the week.

Leadership Debrief and Exercises

The world is crying for innovation and innovators. Occasionally, innovation comes out of a spark of pure genius. However, most of the time, it is born of collaboration, where ideas are discussed openly, freely, and in a place of safety. Southcentral Foundation, Kaas Tailored, and Virginia Mason seem to understand that creating new knowledge and information is not an additive process. They do not have a process for innovation. What they have is systems of leadership where new ideas are respected, welcomed, and valued. Their workforces, by right of being human, already have ideas on how to improve and innovate.

It's a lot like farming—you prepare the soil, buy seed with the best genetics for your soil, and water the fields. But you cannot make the corn grow—you prepare the soil and let nature take its course.

The question is: What are you doing to cultivate innovation? Write down three to five specific, intentional ideas for engineering a culture of innovation.

_____

_____

_____

_____

_____

_____

Take your list to your team and ask them if they agree. Ask them what they think innovation looks like. Ask if they feel their ideas are welcomed and can be discussed openly, free of judgment, so they can grow and flourish.

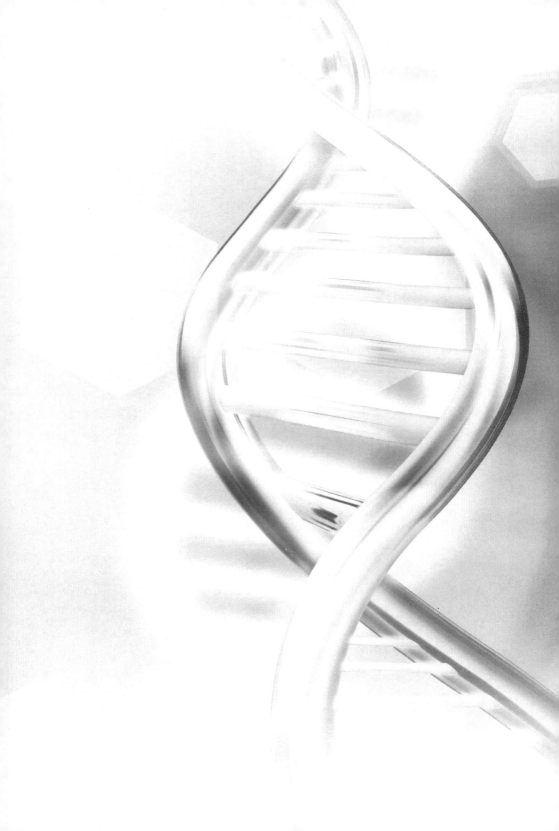

SECTION 3
HARDWIRING THE GENETIC CODE

"Every system is perfectly designed to get the result that it does."

— W. Edwards Deming

In the previous section, we tackled the issue of becoming a DDO—Deliberately Developmental Organization. To maximize value creation, DDOs have a clearly designed process for developing people, maximizing economic value for their customers, and developing cultures of everyday innovation. Then they train every leader on exactly how to do this kind of development. These high-performing teams do not rely on the goodwill of a few leaders. Nor do they rely on personal inspiration or the force of a charismatic personality.

So much of contemporary leadership development defies simple, elementary school math that predicts collaboration and workforce empowerment will be ineffective for organizational transformation. In systems where emerging leaders are selected for their first management position and two thirds of them receive no training, coaching, or mentoring, we are left with books, speeches, and classes on leadership that are provided to individuals separate from and disconnected from organizational missions and culture.

In contrast, high-performing organizations design training for emerging leaders so they will be successful leaders in their unique organizations. One reason the US Army is so successful at developing leaders is they start leadership training in boot camp, and it is not theoretical generalized training out of a library textbook. It is training in leadership the way the Army wants their leaders to lead. In Chapter 6, I wrote about General Barry McCaffrey losing his chief of staff due to a promotion three weeks before engaging the Iraqi army in one of the most complex maneuvers in recent military history. A week later, the chief of staff's replacement arrived, stepped into the job, and performed "flawlessly." This can only happen because Army training is designed specifically to the requirements of the Army—not the Navy or a nonprofit serving the homeless. The Army hardwires its training, integrating it into soldiers' DNA so that every officer knows exactly how to fulfill the requirements of their specific rank. In this section and the following chapters, I will demonstrate how great organizations hardwire their genetic codes to form systems that allow/require all leaders to pull in the same direction and with the same cadence.

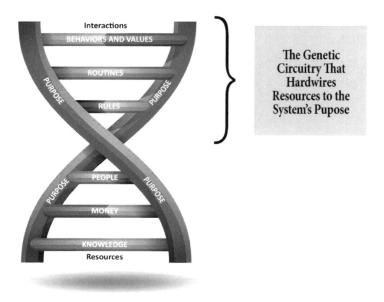

The Genetic Circuitry That Hardwires Resources to the System's Pupose

***

Erin was born in a rural, blue-collar logging community. Her father was the attorney for the local hospital, city, and school. Consequently, she could not do much without her parents knowing about it. She was one of five children, and by her own admission, not the smartest, but certainly the most social. Nor was she the compliant one. As she said, "I was always the kid asking why and needing to understand. If a teacher said I was to memorize this rule or that rule, and could not tell me why, I didn't. This made math really challenging for me because I was just not into memorizing rules."

Although Erin told me she was not a typical rebellious teenager, I have my suspicions that her parents might mildly disagree. She told me a funny story about her family: "I was having a fight with my parents, as usual, and he (older brother) pulls me aside and tells me to 'just play the game.' And I was like, 'What do you mean?' He said, 'Just tell them what they want to hear.' And I was like, 'I don't know how to play the game.'"

Even though she tested out as academically gifted, Erin barely graduated from high school with a GPA high enough to get into college. She ruled out large state schools because she refused to attend a school where the instructors would never know her name. She had no idea what she wanted to study, but she liked kids. She was always babysitting, so she thought education might be a good option—that is until she actually got into a classroom.

Her senior year of college, for her student teaching experience, Erin was assigned an elementary school where 95 percent of students qualified for free or reduced (price) lunch. This is a nice way of saying the school was in an impoverished neighborhood with high unemployment, high drug and alcohol use, and low academic achievement. She was twenty-one, soon to be married, and placed in a portable class-room with thirty-two fourth graders. During her student teaching, one student died from neglect and another was being molested. Erin made multiple calls to Child Protection Services. It was an academic and social war zone. Most days, she cried on her way home.

When her student teaching was completed, Erin had "had it" with education. She had no idea what else she might like to do, but whatever it was, it was not going to be in a classroom. However, something about being newly married and needing a job can change your perspective. Although Erin did not apply for a single teaching job, a friend called just before school started in the fall to tell her about a teaching job that would fit her perfectly. "Would you mind if I gave the principal your name?" the friend asked. Erin agreed, and before she had even filled out an application, the principal called to ask if she could come in for an interview. She agreed but did nothing to prepare.

Erin thought she miserably failed the interview, so she was surprised when the principal called to offer her the job. Feeling like she could do *anything* for a year and needing the money, she found herself back in the classroom. One year turned into two, which turned into seven. Her principal and supervisors quickly saw her talent and encouraged her to get her master's degree and become board certified. Within a few years, she was pushed to take on larger roles. She turned every offer down because, ironically, she now loved the classroom. She finally accepted a different role because she did not want to be rude to her supervisors. That role turned into another (again reluctantly accepted), until finally, it was her turn to try being principal.

Erin had two offers. One from a school in an affluent neighborhood with high income families and high academic expectations. The other in a highly diverse neighborhood with low incomes and a high percentage of students living in poverty.

True to form, she took the latter.

The school was failing on multiple levels. The previous principal had been pushed out by the teachers' union. The school was among the worst academic performers in the district, and rumors about open hostility among the staff were rampant.

Five years later, it was one of the highest-performing schools in the district, and when that was not good enough, it stepped it up another level, becoming the only school in the district to close the achievement gap for two consecutive years.

The morning I sat down with Erin, I said I wanted to learn about her approach to leadership.

Looking away, she said, "Leadership? I don't know anything about leadership."

She then went on to describe the most elegant system of leadership I have found outside the US Army. When I asked if she could give me one or two words that best described her approach, she paused for a second, and said, "This won't be very popular, but love and grace."

My initial thought was, "How nice."

Just outside her door, 450 elementary school children were preparing for one of the last days of school before summer recess. I liked that those children had a principal who loved them. She read my mind.

"I understand what these words mean from a spiritual perspective, but that is not how I use them. To me, they mean a willingness to push people, but in love. It means accountability in love; it means having difficult conversations before staff situations erupt."

Erin went on to detail a system of leadership that focused on love and grace as the path to collaboration. She felt strongly that collaboration between her staff, neighborhood families, and even neighborhood community groups was the key to academic achievement. Love and grace became one side of her double helix; collaboration was the other.

When Erin accepted the appointment as principal, she pulled her entire educational team together, even the custodians, and designed a set of operating rules. Then she challenged the status quo, designing new routines that could have put her at odds with the teachers' union (they did not), and together, she and her staff established a charter that addressed the key behavioral requirements of a successful school—mapping out the circuitry of its genetic code, if you will.

We talked at length about her system, but the concept of grace never came up again, so toward the end of the conversation, I had to ask, "What about grace?"

She pulled back the sleeve of her blouse and showed me the word "grace" tattooed on her wrist. "This," she said, "is how we do innovation."

Erin explained that it takes ten years for a good innovative idea to get out of the halls of academia, go through all the research, and finally get into the classroom. She said, "When the lives of children are at stake, ten years is too long." Furthermore, innovation is a challenge in education because if a great idea fails, that lost time can never be recovered. When a teacher spends two weeks teaching math to fourth graders in a new way, and it fails, that is two weeks lost. It can never be regained. "We just have to learn that sometimes a great idea just does not work, and we have to forgive ourselves." As she said this, she pointed to multiple tissue boxes strategically placed around her office.

In the following chapters, I will describe how Erin's system coded rules, routines, and behaviors to create a cultural DNA that is now hardwired into her school's leadership. This code became the DNA common to her key resources—people, money, and knowledge—and to her purpose of collaboration through love and grace.

I am confident Erin's system could be reproduced in any school in the nation.

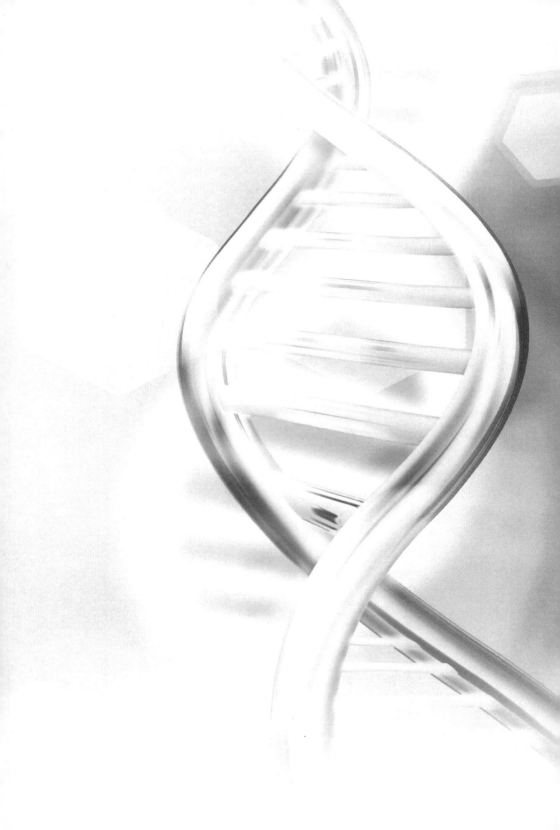

CHAPTER 9

DESIGNING RULES THAT MATTER

"There are no rules here—we're trying to accomplish something."
— Thomas Edison

Rules, routines, and behaviors—these create the genetic circuitry that integrates organizational resources to the larger purpose or function of leadership. With all due respect to Mr. Edison, his statement about there being "no rules" is, in fact, a rule. But his point that rules kill innovation and creativity is correct. The challenge is navigating the swamp of written and unwritten rules.

Some rules are appropriate. Rules that govern sexual and racial harassment are appropriate and necessary. These are the easy ones. Other rules are just bizarre. The first consulting firm I worked for had a rule that no personal affects should be visible in personal workspaces. Evidently, they did not want family photos laying around. Of course, no one paid attention to this rule and put all the family photos they wanted in their personal workspaces.

The dangerous rules, those that carry the most power, are the unwritten rules. For example, I spent several years working for a regional consulting firm. Every morning, the president would walk into his office, shut and lock the door, pull the interior window shades down, and do his own work. At noon, he would reappear, go to lunch, and when he came back, he would raise the blinds in his office, open his door, and make himself available to anyone who needed to see him. There was no rule that said, "Don't bother David in the morning," but it was pretty clear we should never bother David in the morning.

Rules and the ability to make them is a source of power. If I had walked into my office in the morning, closed the interior blinds, and locked my door, nobody would have paid attention. Especially not my boss. But because one of the senior partners and the president of the company did this, everyone noticed and knew not to knock.

Rules of genetics govern how the basic elements of a DNA molecule interact. For example, Adenine is always paired with Thymine, not Guanine. In the same way, rules determine how basic organizational resources—people, money, knowledge—interact. But it is not just the rule itself, but the source of the rule that creates organizational power. In *Thinking in Systems: A Primer*, Donella Meadows says, "(Rules) are high leverage points. Power over the rules is real power.... If you want to understand the deepest malfunctions of systems, pay attention to the rules and to who has power over them."[26]

When Erin brought up the subject of rules, she immediately had my attention. Her process of developing rules was as important as the rules themselves. When Erin came to this elementary school, it was a mess. In response, Erin did something I thought was brilliant.

Before school started in the fall, Erin brought in a facilitator and arranged a meeting of her entire team. They identified every rule that governed how they interacted. There were good rules and bad rules. They even identified the absence of a rule when there should be one. Every rule was written on posters for all to see and digest. Then Erin

---

26 Meadows, Donella H. Thinking in Systems: A Primer. White River Junction, VT: Chelsea Green Publishing. Kindle Edition, 2008. Kindle location 2871.

told her team, "Now, let's rewrite our own rules."

They began to write a set of rules that supported a culture of collaboration in a spirit of love and grace. Erin said, "We went around popcorn style identifying the rules of how we would engage each other to create an experience of collaboration. We did not stop until we didn't have anything left to say."

These new rules were incorporated into a charter, which had a dual effect on Erin's ability to lead her team:

1. The power of the rules came from the team behind them. They were not just Erin's; they were the team's rules. Because the entire team developed the rules, anyone who chose not to work by them essentially took themselves off the team.

2. When Erin needed to have one of those difficult conversations with a member of her staff, the rules provided her with a framework for the discussion. Erin was just enforcing the team's rules.

There was also an unintended benefit to these rules and the other parts of Erin's system. Erin's system attracted higher quality teachers. Word gets around, and the best teachers wanted to work in a system where collaboration was important, expectations were high, and innovation was respected. When teachers transferred to different schools or were encouraged to move on, they were often replaced by teachers with greater passions for education. The result—in seven years this elementary school went from failure to closing the achievement gap—a massive transformation.

How Rules Effect Leadership in the US Army

I first heard General Barry McCaffrey speak at a lunch hosted by the Salvation Army. As a member of the advisory board, I was invited and anxious to hear the general speak. Toward the end of his talk, McCaffrey spoke about decentralizing leadership and command. My reaction was, *This is the most bizarre thing I have ever heard—a four-star general telling the world to decentralize leadership."*

During the question and answer time, I asked McCaffrey how the US Army decentralizes leadership. His one-word answer was "Training." He explained that training to the specific requirements of the job or rank removed the need for micromanagement.

Later, when I interviewed McCaffrey, he explained that even for a four-star general, the rule was he could give a direct order to a direct report or an officer one level down. Similarly, a two-star general could give an order to a direct report or someone one level below. This rule protects one of the Army's core values, an idea intricate to their DNA—the soldier closest to the problem or battle is in the best position to execute a solution.

For example, McCaffrey told me how he had been in the White House Situation Room several times, watching a military operation through the magic of satellite technology and linked communications. "We had virtually as much information as the soldiers on the ground and could have given orders to the commanding officer." Yet the rule is the soldier closest to the mission makes the decisions. He said, "If you want to really screw up a mission, take the decision-making power away from the soldier who is on the ground." (Actually, his language was way more colorful.)

When I asked McCaffrey how the US Army approaches leadership, his immediate response was, "We practice servant leadership." My follow-up was: How does the Army implement servant leadership? He gave me two simple examples. As he was explaining, my mind went to two very popular movies. In the 1986, best picture Oscar-winning film *Platoon*, one scene depicts soldiers standing around a fifty-five-gallon barrel stirring the contents of the latrine (human waste) as it burns with the help of diesel fuel. McCaffrey said this method of waste disposal in combat zones is still practiced. While civilians might assume this delicate task is reserved for the lowest private, the reality is very different. The rule is everyone, even the company commander, takes a turn. As the general explained, leaders participating in the routine reinforces the practice of servant leadership and one of the Army's core values—selfless service—and becomes part of an integrated system of servant leadership.

McCaffrey also described the order in which soldiers and officers get on and off a helicopter into and out of an operation. As he was explaining, I recalled another movie—*We Were Soldiers*, where Mel Gibson plays Lieutenant Colonel Hal Moore. The movie depicts the Battle of Ia Drang. In the final scene, Gibson is the last to board a departing helicopter after a bloody fight with North Vietnamese regulars. While the cinematography is compelling, a larger story, while largely symbolic, reinforces a leader's role—work to ensure the safety of lower-ranking soldiers. The highest-ranking officer is the last to board the helicopter, ensuring all their troops are safely onboard before climbing in themselves.

McCaffrey also described another practice where, in the cafeteria, the highest-ranking officer eats last. The US Marine Corps also has this rule, publicized in Simon Sinek's book, *Leaders Eat Last*.

I asked my nephew, who had just completed thirteen weeks of Marine basic training, who eats last at chow time. With great Marine Corps gusto, he declared, "The highest-ranking officer."

While the practice of leaders going last is simple, it reinforces one of the core values of both the Army and Marine Corps (probably the other services as well)—selfless service is not just a catch phrase for adorning posters. Selfless service is a core value, and rules are in place to support it.

How Rules Support Safety

As I described in Section 1 of this book, when Paul O'Neil took over as CEO of Alcoa in 1987, his appointment was hardly met with jubilation in the financial press. His announcement that his focus would be employee safety did nothing to capture the imaginations of financial analysts and major shareholders. To back this up, O'Neil established a rule—he would be notified within twenty-four hours of every accident resulting in injury that required a day off work. He put teeth in the rule in two more ways:

1. If the rule was broken, the plant manager who failed to inform him would be terminated.

2. O'Neil gave out his personal phone number to any member of the workforce who had an idea for improving safety whose supervisor was not listening.

At a shareholder meeting one day, Sister Mary Margaret, a Benedictine nun, stood up during the question-and-answer session and publicly accused O'Neil of lying about safety. Her acquisition focused on a plant in Mexico. The plant had a good safety record, O'Neil argued, showing her the safety chart for that specific plant. The sister's order owned a whopping fifty shares in Alcoa, but still, O'Neil invited her to his office to discuss her concerns.

When they were done, O'Neil sent the director of human resources and the general counsel to Mexico to find out if there was any truth to Sister Mary Margaret's claim. Turns out, there had been a small release of fumes and some workers had become ill; a few had needed to take time off work, but everyone had recovered within a day or two. The manager solved the problem by installing ventilators. Unfortunately, he did not report the incident to O'Neil. He was one of Alcoa's most capable managers—he was fired anyway.[27]

Rules are important. They make up the leadership system's DNA, producing its purpose. In this case, safety. The result was the best economic performance in Alcoa's history. Safety became the purpose, the lens through which every process and system was evaluated and improved.

People Vs. Machine?

During an interview with Tucker Kaas, Jeff Kaas' son, I asked about rules. Jeff is one of those guys who believes the fewer rules, the better. However, he has one sacred rule: Machines serve people, not the other way around. Tucker told me a story of how one day he was working in the cutting area, where they cut wood frames for their furniture. They had just bought a very expensive, numerically controlled cutting machine. It could make extremely precise cuts, which is important since the company is committed to one-piece flow through its manufacturing system. (In the simplest terms, one-piece flow means parts are moved through the process step-by-step with no work-in-process be-

---

27 Duhigg, Charles. *The Power of Habit*. New York, NY: Random House, 2012. p. 123. Kindle location 1947.

tween either one piece or small batches.) However, after a few weeks, it was clear the machine required extra attention from workers. They sold the machine at a loss because machines serve people, not the other way around. I'm sure their accountant had a heart attack when they saw that transaction.

Rules for Supporting a Leadership of Respect

At Seattle's Virginia Mason Hospital, critical rules drive leadership behavior. At the core of its Lean for Leaders training is the theme, "Go see, ask why, and show respect." This is core to the "genba," a Japanese word for what some have called "management by walking around." The rules are simple enough, but profoundly difficult for the traditional leader to embrace. The leader must become a coach, mentor, learner, and developer of people. They must refrain from solving problems for their staff because it takes away the opportunity for staff to learn, grow, and develop everyday improvement skills. The rule is, instead of being a problem solver, a leader must learn to become a problem framer. They must know how to frame a problem accurately so front line staff can both learn and experience the satisfaction of solving a problem on their own. Allowing members of the workforce to solve problems transfers the satisfaction and confidence from the leader to the worker. In this way, leaders demonstrate respect.

When I interviewed Rhonda Stewart, a transformational sensei at the Virginia Mason Institute and co-creator of the Lean for Leaders curriculum, she spoke of the challenge and reward in this kind of leadership system. She explained how some leaders are strong, confident, problem solvers—the traditional model of a great leader—but find great difficulty leading in a Lean environment. Every bit of these leaders' recognition has come from being great problem solvers. In this system, they have to turn that off. Leaders must learn to coach workers in problem solving. On the other hand, she said, "We see front line workers who often lacked confidence and were afraid to speak up, absolutely blossom." I asked her if the hospital required an open door policy—a policy often considered a characteristic of great leaders. Stewart said an open door policy would indicate a leader is not leading the way the hospital requires. Leaders are to be out with their staff, coaching and mentoring, not uselessly sitting in an office.

A Most Unusual Case Study

When I began to understand what leadership systems looked like, I began to see them in the most unlikely places. In the late 1920s and early 1930s, New York crime was controlled by five "families." Unfortunately, they were frequently competing for similar "business" and the result was war. Dead bodies showed up in the streets of New York at astonishing rates. The gangster Charles "Lucky" Luciano decided there was a better way to do business. He convinced his competitors it was better to work together than compete against each other. The result was the formation of the "Commission," which basically acted like a board of directors governing the five crime families. Lucky and the Commission established a set of rules for all members, and these rules governed a wide array of leadership behaviors. Things like leadership succession and women who were off limits, like wives of family members.

The rules, as I discovered, were designed to do one primary thing: protect the family, the system's primary purpose. Consequences for breaking the rules were severe. For example, you could not "whack" (murder) a family member without authorization from the Commission. Consequently, the five families lived in peace (at least with each other) and la Costra Nostra (the New York Mafia) became so strong that many considered it a shadow government. In fact, estimates indicate the Mafia was the largest NGO (Non-Governmental Agency) in the nation, yet the FBI either would or could not acknowledge they existed until the mid-1960s.

At the zenith of their power, the Mafia controlled virtually all construction in New York City, all major unions, and of course, alcohol, prostitution, and gambling. However, its downfall came when the Commission failed to enforce one of its own rules.

In 1985, John Gotti, Jr. whacked his superior without authorization. The Commission then failed to enforce its own rule, which called for them to execute Gotti. Consequently, trust was broken. When "Made Men" could not trust the system, they began talking to local and national law enforcement. The infamous la Costra Nostra crumbled from within.

Summary

When Erin worked with her team collaboratively to design the rules that would govern how they would all work together to help students prosper academically, she gave away a lot of her personal power. This took courage and confidence in her team. It also took courage to enforce rules designed by the team.

Like you, I have read a lot of books and heard many inspirational talks about courageous leadership. Churchill's famous, "We will fight on the beaches…" speech after a near disaster at Dunkirk comes to mind. However, that kind of courage only comes along once or twice in a generation. Erin's courage is a little more pedestrian, but no less important.

What impressed me was her confidence in her team. By working with them in collaboration, not only was she transferring power, but she was demonstrating confidence in a team that, the year before, had produced sub-par academic results. Captain David Marquet of the *USS Santa Fe* did the same when he determined that the ship's poor performance was not the result of an inept workforce, but an outdated system of leadership that focused on followers turning off their brains in favor of being told what to do.

Erin and Marquet created systems that were relatively small in scale. However, Virginia Mason is a highly complex organization with more than 9,500 employees. Yet by designing a scalable system, they produced enviable results. Transferring power from individual leaders to teams requires confidence in those teams and the courage to enforce the rules that support the system.

In the next chapter, we will learn how Erin and others incorporated innovative, yet incredibly simple routines to drive workforce innovation and engagement.

Leadership Debrief and Exercises

Do these exercises yourself first. Then follow up with your team.

1. Make a list of at least ten to fifteen unwritten rules that govern the way you operate as a team or organization. Don't bother with the written rules; those are a given. Focus on the unwritten rules that make up your culture.

    _____

    _____

    _____

_____

_____

_____

_____

_____

_____

_____

_____

_____

_____

2. Map or align each rule to your established purpose or outcome of your leadership or at least to your core values. For example, if the rule (probably unwritten) says that the workforce goes to the manager's office to find a solution to a problem, does this support a purpose of respect? Or of collaboration? Or of safety? Should the rule be the reverse? Which rules support the primary purpose of your leadership? What would happen if you intentionally discarded all the others? Do you have rules that support or inhibit psychological safety among your team?

_____

_____

_____

_____

_____

_____

_____

_____

_____

_____

_____

_____

_____

_____

3. What other rules should you adopt to support your primary purpose or core values?

_____

_____

_____

_____

_____

_____

_____

_____

4. Repeat the exercise with your team, but do *not* start with your own rules. Let them go through the exercise without being prejudiced by yours.

_____

_____

_____

_____

_____

_____

_____

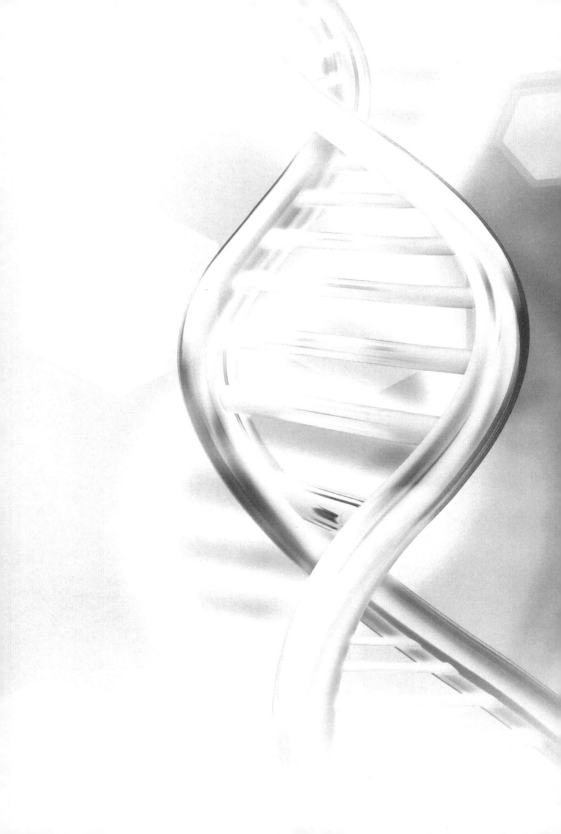

CHAPTER 10

DESIGNING ROUTINES AND HABITS

"We are what we repeatedly do. Excellence,
then, is not an act, but a habit."

— Aristotle

It is Tuesday morning—7:00 a.m. exactly. The executive team at Seattle's Virginia Mason Hospital begins a weekly review of its progress toward the hospital's strategic initiatives. The most interesting part of the process is invisible to outside observers who might expect to see high level executives sitting around a custom-crafted conference table, enjoying French pastries, coffee served in porcelain china, and a view of Seattle's harbor from a penthouse executive suite. In fact, the executives are in a rather drab hallway, reviewing data displayed on a simple paper graph that takes up twenty feet of the wall.

This weekly ritual reflects the daily rhythms of an award-winning hospital recognized as one of the safest in America. This weekly gathering has some rules: 1) do not be late, 2) meet every Tuesday morning, and 3) no sitting down.

Everyone stands. These routines and the rules that accompany them create the genetic code that sequences the leadership system's DNA, coding it to its purpose—in this case, respect. While average organizations allow these routines to evolve over time with little thought to their value, organizations that achieve and sustain elite performance design their routines. They are what Charles Duhigg, author of the bestseller, *The Power of Habit*, calls "keystone habits." They create institutional muscle memory in the same way an Olympic athlete creates muscle memory by constant practice, practice, and more practice.

***

It is a time-honored tradition, and for most, a regulatory requirement that schoolteachers receive an annual evaluation. Nothing is wrong with this practice. It is a routine that provides feedback and opportunities for development and professional growth. Except Principal Erin determined it was really inadequate in building a culture of collaboration and institutional learning. While she could not abandon the annual evaluation, she augmented it with a process of peer review and observation. In this way, a third-grade teacher might watch a fifth-grade teacher teach math. Or a fourth-grade teacher might observe a second-grade teacher teach English grammar.

Being observed can be tense, and to some extent, it probably caused tension among the teachers. Culturally, teachers are considered educational leaders and the classroom tends to be their sacred domain. But Erin understood peer review could also create opportunities for coaching and mentoring. A more experienced teacher might coach a less experienced teacher or even the reverse. A teacher just coming out of college might have a better perspective on the latest best practices in teaching science than a teacher who has been doing it for twenty years.

Part of Erin's personal leadership style was to know her teachers well enough to know their passions. When a teacher is passionate about teaching math, they enjoy the opportunity of coaching a teacher who is passionate about language but not so much about teaching math.

The new routine was not about personal performance in the classroom, but about engaging teachers with their passions to the benefit of students. The result was a win-win solution for both teachers and students.

And because the system made it clear the objective was collaboration, growth, learning, and student outcomes, the teachers' union remained silent. Furthermore, by transferring power to her team and demonstrating confidence in them, Erin built their trust.

In their book based on ten years of research, *Evolutionary Theory of Economic Change*, Yale professors Richard Nelson and Sidney Winter concluded that organizations were creatures of routines, and their routines would determine their behavior over time. They state:

> "In our evolutionary [organizational] theory, these routines play the role that genes play in biological evolutionary theory. They are a persistent feature of the organism [or enterprise] and determine its possible behavior."[28]

When Erin designed a new routine for her school, she was doing more than just tinkering at the fringes of academic achievement. She was innovating educational culture and the system that has the power to close achievement gaps. In short, she was engineering the DNA of a culture of collaboration in a quest for high quality education for all students.

---

28 Nelson, Richard and Sidney Winter. *An Evolutionary Theory of Economic Change*. Cambridge, MA: Harvard UP, 1982. p. 14.

How Routines Hardwire Healthcare Performance

As previously mentioned, the Malcolm Baldrige National Quality Award is the nation's highest award for organizational performance. Many organizations seeking this elite honor take seven to ten years to achieve it. To win one Baldrige award is a huge achievement. To win multiple awards is massive. John Heer is the only leader to have taken three different organizations to the national awards ceremony. The last was when he was CEO of North Mississippi Health Services.

North Mississippi Health Services (NMHS) is in Tupelo, Mississippi, in the northeast corner of the state. It draws patients and customers from twenty-four rural counties in both Mississippi and Alabama. The community-owned healthcare system has accepted a huge challenge—improving the health of the population it serves, not just services to individual patients. NMHS serves a population that is among the poorest, least educated, and least healthy in the US. It is not enough to stitch up a wound; NMHS seeks to address the wound's cause. Frequently, patients end up at NMHS because of long-practiced, unhealthy lifestyles leading to chronic disease.

John Heer joined NMHS in 2004, and he was later appointed as its CEO. When he took over as CEO, no designed leadership system existed. Every leader operated according to their own values and understanding of how to lead. Consequently, there was infighting between departments and leadership. The NMHS board wanted something different. In an interview, John explained that his first step was to gain the board's approval of his approach. They would use the Baldrige Excellence Framework as their guide for innovation, transformation, better patient care, and a happier workforce. John's second step was one few leaders have ever taken: he designed a leadership system from the ground up based on the principles of servant leadership.

John started by identifying the core requirements of the system:

1. It must have a clear purpose: i.e., leaders are servants who will create an engaged workforce.
2. It needed a set of behaviors, routines, and rules (standard work) that supported this purpose.

As John's system came online, he initiated several new routines for his leaders and made these new routines *the* priority. For example, he required leader *rounding*. Much like Virginia Mason in Seattle (where they call it genba) leaders at NMHS were required to make rounds, talking with workers and generally making themselves available to the workforce. Everything else on their schedule was secondary to this priority.

The routine of rounding became like a genetic coding that hardwired the system of servant leadership. John wanted his leaders to work *with* their staff rather than sit in an office waiting for their staff to come to them with problems. In researching John and NMHS, I came across several stories about his management style. The joke was that if anyone ever needed to see John, they should not bother going to his office. He was seldom there. You needed to track him down because he was always wandering around the hospital and clinics learning what was going on, how he could assist, and how he could help those serving the patients and creating everyday value.

John also had a personal routine that supported being a servant leader. He took every opportunity to eat lunch in one of the cafeterias. He explained he could learn more about what was going on in the hospital in thirty minutes eating lunch with the nurses, aides, and administrators than he ever could in a staff meeting.

John wanted his system to produce servant leaders. From this platform, they would generate workforce engagement that would increase patient satisfaction. The data indicates the system worked as designed. For example, NMHS was:

- The 2012 recipient of the Malcolm Baldrige National Quality Award in the healthcare category.

- In the 96th percentile in workforce engagement nationally.

- In the 90th percentile in patient satisfaction nationally.

- At a 9 percent turnover ratio of nurses (national average is 25 percent).

- Among *Fortune Magazine's* Top 100 Companies to Work For for three straight years.

- Named the number one hospital in Press Ganey's patient-satisfaction database for five straight years.

- Named Performance Improvement Leaders Top 100 Hospitals for three straight years.

***

I heard a similar story about another hospital CEO who brings trust and a hands-on touch to his organization during one of my first interviews for this book. Steve is the Medical Director of a Level 1 Emergency Department that serves a three-state region. He told me about working with a prior CEO who seldom left the executive floor and mostly communicated via email. Even though Steve was a member of the executive team, he seldom had any contact with the CEO outside of formal meetings and email. Consequently, little basis existed for trust in the chief executive officer. When that CEO moved on, the new CEO came onboard and immediately moved his office from the executive floor to the first floor, right behind the admitting center. From this location, he could get a better feel for the pulse and rhythms of this large, urban county hospital serving some of the most venerable populations in the region.

As Steve explained, the new CEO visited the emergency department two to three times a week just to see how things were going, ensure everyone had what they needed, and acknowledge the good work the team was doing. The result? Names turned into faces, relationships were established, trust was built, and engagement soared.

Leader rounding, or daily genba, is a simple routine that takes little training. It does not require a PhD in organizational systems or theory. It just requires leaders to get out of their offices and learn how they can support their staff.

Hardwiring Routines in Manufacturing

As reported earlier, Paul O'Neil took a rather unconventional path to corporate growth. Instead of focusing on market share, earnings, and quality, he focused on employee safety. This made safety the lens through which every process and system in this international manufacturing giant could be evaluated. In doing so, he was able to release the basic human capacity for creativity, innovation, transformation, and in his case, safety. To do this, he established several new routines to reinforce the purpose of employee safety. I think they are worth repeating here:

- All accidents must be reported to O'Neil within twenty-four hours (rule).

- The accident report must include an action plan to prevent similar accidents (rule).

- Failure to comply would result in immediate dismissal (rule).

- Safety audits were made as important as financial audits.

- Corporate meetings, including board meetings, started with employee safety reports and a reminder to everyone that safety was critically important—instead of the usual summaries of financial performance.

***

Jeff Kaas at Kaas Tailored has done the same thing with *kaizen*. He made it so routine that it became part of the company's institutional muscle memory. I observed something else when I visited Kaas Tailored that speaks to the power of routine, leadership, and strategy. Because it has no offices or conference rooms with the usual whiteboards where leaders and staff can gather and problem solve, it put whiteboards everywhere. But not the usual boards hung on a wall. The company has entire movable walls made out of whiteboard material. They have tables made out of whiteboard material, and when a wall is structural, they have sprayed white board-type coating on the walls. They want leaders and staff to be able to problem solve immediately, close to the tools they need to illustrate the problem. Colored markers are everywhere. When I sat down with Jeff's son Tucker, we sat at a small, round table in the middle of the production floor, and the table was made out of whiteboard material. As Tucker responded to my questions, he did not just tell me a story; he drew pictures on the table.

Simple Routines Hardwire Military Leadership

When Captain Dave Marquet took over command of the *USS Santa Fe*, he had to start from scratch, designing a new system of leadership from a very old and traditional model. In virtually every metric, his submarine was at the bottom of the fleet. Marquet's commanding officer gave him the flexibility to design a new way of leading, one that would engage all 135 crew members.

In *Turn the Ship Around*, Marquet wrote about establishing a new routine called "take deliberate action." This routine required sailors to pause and vocalize what they were about to do before doing it. Marquet was inspired to create this routine after an incident shutting down the reactor and hooking the submarine up to shore electrical power. While nothing bad happened, it could have been a disaster. Instead of punishing those involved, he used the event as a learning opportunity, and in doing so, established a new routine. It became a keystone habit aboard the *Santa Fe*. "Take deliberate action," created institutional muscle memory that forced sailors to slow down so they were not on autopilot with the associated risk of making a very bad decision—something that could be deadly when cruising the ocean's depths.

But Marquet also established other routines that turned the ship from the worst-performing ship in the fleet to the highest. When the ship was preparing for inspections prior to deployment, the crew initiated the "three name rule." (Okay, I guess this is a rule and a routine.) The routine was to identify three names in greeting a guest inspector. Marquet describes it as going something like this, "Good morning, Commodore Kenny, my name is Petty Officer Jones, welcome aboard *Santa Fe*."[29]

---

29 Marquet, L. David. *Turn the Ship Around!* New York, NY: Penguin Publishing Group. Kindle Edition, 2012. Kindle location 1152.

After the first inspection under his command, Marquet was initially disappointed. Only about 10 percent of his sailors followed through with the routine the first time. However, the new routine did not go unnoticed by the inspectors. Within the inspection report, which gave the ship the best score in its history, the three-name rule was mentioned. The crew of the *USS Santa Fe* were on their way to moving from the bottom to number one in performance.

As I referenced in the last chapter, the US Army and Marines both have a routine that the highest-ranking officer eats last. The rule is that they eat last; the routine is that they follow through. When I asked my nephew the Marine how often officers ate last, he said, "All the time." In thirteen weeks of basic training, he never saw an officer get food before a lower-ranking officer, enlisted Marine, or even a recruit. While simple, this routine reinforces the purpose, focus, and goal of servant leadership and selfless service. For the Army, it is a practical way officers demonstrate one of the core values of the US Army: Put the welfare of the nation, the Army, and your subordinates before your own. Requiring the highest-ranking officer to be the last to board a helicopter and the first to get off is another example of a "keystone habit" that codes the system's genetics to the purpose of leadership.

Summary

When Erin established a new routine of peer review, she was taking a bold step that she hoped would improve learning for 450 elementary school children. It was not an activity without risk, but she tied it to her purpose of collaboration. In doing so, she created a "keystone habit" that created the genes and built the DNA of her team leading to the larger goal of academic achievement for all students. Establishing a new routine may involve some risk. However, most routines are simple, yet profoundly powerful. When an Army private sees the company commander taking his turn to stir a pot of burning human waste, it says something. When medical assistants, nurses, dishwashers, and emergency room specialists see the hospital CEO coming around and showing an interest in their work, it says something. It builds trust. It builds engagement.

Designing regular routines to be "keystone habits" becomes part of the genetic code of leadership. Routines become the organization's DNA, hardwiring resources to the larger purpose of leadership. As Marquet observed, the math just works better if there are 135 active and engaged sailors on a nuclear-powered attack submarine than just one doing all the thinking and giving orders to the remaining 134. Herein lies the opportunity. Changing the way leaders lead, using simple routines to sequence the system's genes (resources) to its larger purpose, will unleash the creative energy of millions of healthcare workers, educators, and manufacturing employees.

Every place I found an organization routinely operating at an elite level, I found simple routines that set the daily rhythms of excellent performance. Routines that matter are usually simple. They require no special training or advanced education. I like the way Admiral William H. McRaven put it in his 2014 commencement address to the graduates of the University of Texas at Austin, "If you want to change the world, start off by making your bed."

Rules and routines are two genes that create organizational DNA in a leadership system. The third gene is human behavior. Every time I found a designed leadership system, I found an organization that took human behavior out of the clothes closet and put it front and center for all to see.

Leadership Debrief and Exercises

Think for a few minutes about your daily routines. What do you do habitually, without thinking about it? What do you do when you come into the office? Do you greet your team or just walk by them?

Identify five to ten daily, weekly, or monthly work routines. Write each down on a card or Post-it-note. Let them sit on your desk for a few days and see if they change as you observe yourself.

Like you previously did with the rules, map each routine to your primary purpose as a leader or to your organizational core values. Which ones support them, and which ones inhibit them? Think about your staff. How do your routines affect them? Do they encourage? Do they discourage? Do your routines cultivate a culture, an environment,

_____

_____

_____

_____

_____

_____

_____

Repeat this exercise with your staff but do not let them see your set of routines.

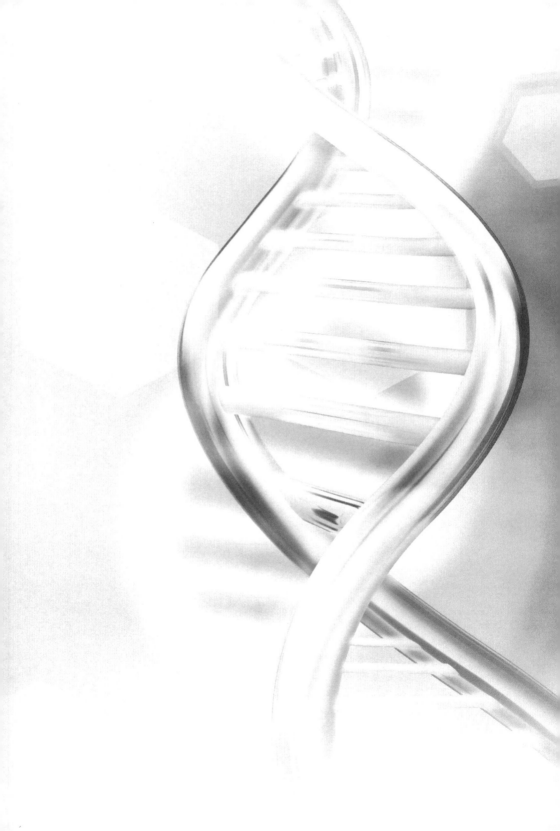

CHAPTER 11

DESIGNING SYSTEM BEHAVIORS

"Behavior drives people—people drive business."

— Anonymous

Rules, routines, and human behaviors—together they create the genetic code that connects organizational resources to the purpose of leadership. Eileen Branscome is a forty-year veteran of the healthcare industry. She recently retired as the Chief Operating Officer (COO) of Mason General Hospital and Family of Clinics, a rural hospital system in western Washington. She started out as a nurse and moved up the ranks while working her way across the nation a few times. She has seen it all and done it all.

Eileen is equal parts kind, thoughtful, caring, compassionate, and ferociously determined to provide the best care possible for her patients and community. One of her favorite sayings is that healthcare was built on the backs of courageous, rule-breaking women. She is the perfect embodiment of this. By her own admission, she has been fired more times than she can count, mostly for refusing to submit to oversized medical egos with overblown opinions of personal importance.

One of my favorite "Eileen" stories is when she was in charge of a Midwest hospital's operating room. A surgeon was having a bad day, got angry, threw a temper tantrum, and with it a scalpel, which went sailing right by her head. Eileen quietly informed the irate surgeon that she could throw a scalpel better and with greater accuracy. No more scalpels were thrown while Eileen oversaw the OR.

In a 2016 *Harvard Business Review* article, the authors argued convincingly that the next wave of innovation in the operating room—innovation that will make patients safer—will not be technical, but will address behavior and the way people interact. They state, "Pay attention [to] how individuals interact with one another and organize their day-to-day work...but also to the actual behaviors, practices, and interactions that unfold between people as they care for patients and manage the organization."[30]

✳✳✳

One thing that surprised me while conducting the research for this book was how much emphasis high-performing organizations put on their leaders' personal behavior. During my interview with Erin, the subject of behavior naturally flowed into the conversation. What struck me, though, was that by starting out with a focus on collaboration, she and her team set the framework for working and interacting with one another so that collaboration would flourish. Also, there was no denying the strong connection between behavior within her team and the team members' personal feelings. The following chart outlines just two parts of the charter Erin and her team developed.

---

30 Ghaferi, Amir A. et al. "The Next Wave of Hospital Innovation to Make Patients Safer." *Harvard Business Review.* (August 8, 2016).

KEY FEELING	DEFINITION	KEY WORDS OR BEHAVIORS
Optimistically hopeful	To feel optimistically hopeful, we will use positive statements and keep our lens optimistic. We will smile. We will focus on goals by creating a plan and adjusting it as needed on our way toward our goal. We will be persistent. We will be solution-based in our planning and interactions. To create a positive environment, we will interpret people's words and actions in a positive way, reframing for the positive when necessary. We will also give all parties an opportunity to talk and share their ideas.	• Positive statements • Smile • Creating plans • Adjusting plans • Interpret actions of others positively • Give others opportunity to talk and share their ideas

KEY FEELING	DEFINITION	KEY WORDS OR BEHAVIORS
Cohesive	To feel cohesive, we realize and acknowledge that all students are OUR students. We will take the time to meet and talk to one another as a partner, team, and staff—both formally and informally. In meetings, we will hold ourselves accountable for participation. We will support one another when things are not going well. This means we will provide support by taking the time to send an email or talk with a colleague, and we will accept support when someone offers it. We will keep the commitment to working together as one of our goals.	• All students are OUR students • Take time to partner • Hold ourselves accountable • We will support and we will accept support • Committed to working together

Erin explained that in creating their charter, they spent a lot of time on the idea of being optimistic. It was not just the idea that her team needed to behave optimistically; it was that they wanted to *feel* optimistic. Eventually, it was revised to "optimistically hopeful." Working with students from broad ethnic and economic backgrounds, the teachers wanted to feel optimistically hopeful that they were contributing to something worthwhile and important. I think we call this feeling "engagement." What I thought was so brilliant was that Erin did not create these behaviors out of her own set of prescribed personal values. Her team created them, and then defined each for their unique organization. The other thing that impressed me with this charter is that there is no big "I" in there. It is all focused on creating a culture of collaboration that benefits their students.

You may find reading about behaviors and feelings to feel a little "squishy." In a fast-paced, competitive economy, personal feeling get pushed aside by the demand for results. Yet I think Erin and her team stumbled onto a reality that is true of all high-performing teams—psychological safety.

In 2012, Google, arguably one of the most innovative companies operating in a fast, competitive environment, began a formal project to study why some of its teams consistently outperformed others. It was code-named Project Aristotle. The researchers studied 180 different teams and mined mountains of data. However, in a company known for its ability to see trends, they found little to work with.

Parallel to their internal research, they were also looking outside the company. When they discovered the concept of "psychological safety," their own data started to make sense. Their conclusion was that the number one determinate of team performance was whether or not individual members *felt* psychologically safe.

In his book *The 4 Stages of Psychological Safety*, Dr. Timothy Clark defines psychological safety as, "A condition in which you feel: 1) included, 2) safe to learn, 3) safe to contribute, and 4) safe to challenge the status quo—all without fear of being embarrassed, marginalized, or punished in some way."[31] I think what Erin and her team did was identify those behaviors and group norms that created a culture of psychological safety. Erin's job, then, became ensuring the continued psychological safety of her staff. The result was they became one of the few schools in the nation to close the achievement gap between rich and poor, majority and minority.

Behavioral Charters in Driving Healthcare

When John Heer took over as CEO of North Mississippi Health Services, he designed a system based on the principles of servant leadership. He determined this model would produce an engaged workforce. In other words, instead of running an organization of six hospitals and thirty-four clinics with the help of 6,999 workers, John designed a system where 7,000 smart, emotionally engaged, and passionate healthcare providers ran six hospitals and thirty-four clinics and managed 576,000 patient visits each year. John did what Marquet did when he took command of the *USS Santa Fe*. Marquet determined the math was more in his favor if he had 135 smart, capable, emotionally engaged sailors running the submarine rather than one captain running the ship and 134 sailors waiting to be told what to do. Only John did it on a much larger scale.

In reading the NMHS application for the 2012 Malcom Baldrige National Quality Award, I was struck by how many times I saw the word "behavior." When I asked John about this, he was very clear that in the system he had designed, all leaders were expected to model eight core behaviors:

---

31 Clark, Timothy. *The 4 Stages of Psychological Safety*. Oakland, CA: Barrett-Koehler Publishers. p. 2.

- Kindness
- Respectfulness
- Selflessness
- Forgiveness
- Honesty
- Commitment
- Being results-oriented/"no excuses"
- Being ego-directed toward team accomplishments

John was not satisfied with creating a list of these behaviors and then posting them on a board in a workroom. He designed a system that required leaders to be responsible for engaging their teams. To do this, he set up a 360-degree evaluation for each leader, including himself, where each would be evaluated by a group of subordinates, peers, and supervisors. This evaluation included modeling these key behaviors. At a minimum of once a year, every leader and manager would receive this feedback evaluation, and if their score was not high enough, the manager would be evaluated twice a year and be provided a coach to help them in areas they were weak. As you can see, the system required leaders to assume a high level of responsibility for their teams.

For example, being "results-oriented, no excuses" and "ego-directed toward team accomplishments" was more than a nice idea. Leaders were evaluated against these behaviors. There was no letting "Pat be Pat in taking credit for the team's accomplishments." John saw the reality of what Jeffery Pfeffer predicted in *Leadership BS* when he said, "When leaders' own jobs and salaries depend on how well they look after others, they will do so. Until then, relying on leaders' generosity of spirit or the exhortations of the leadership literature is an ineffective and risky way to ensure that leaders take care of anyone other than themselves."[32]

---

32 Pfeffer, Jeffrey. Leadership BS: *Fixing Workplaces and Careers One Truth at a Time*. New York, NY: Harper Collins, 2015. p. 168-169.

When I asked how this new system went over with John's leadership team, he laughed and said half his leaders walked out or were encouraged to move on. Those who stayed did so because they thought "This too shall pass." It did not pass. However, those who did stay and those who came on board later had the opportunity to be engaged with a championship-caliber healthcare system.

The US Marine Corps—What Makes Them So Good?

I could not have been prouder of my nephew Jon when he decided to become a Marine. He was following in his grandfather's footsteps— my father-in-law was a twenty-eight-year veteran and Marine Corps Aviator. Within ten days, Jon turned twenty, passed the final fitness test (the famed "crucible"), and graduated as a brand-new United States Marine Corps Private. When he returned home on a ten-day leave, I asked him what he had learned about leadership.

Jon immediately said, "JJ did tie buckle" (JJDIDTIEBUCKLE). I hate acronyms. My initial thought was, *Thirteen weeks of Marine Corps boot camp and the most important thing this kid learned was an acronym?* However, I was curious, so I looked it up:

- Justice
- Judgment
- Dependability
- Initiative
- Decisiveness
- Tact
- Integrity
- Endurance
- Bearing

- Unselfishness
- Courage
- Knowledge

Upon further reflection, I realized that while still a recruit, not even yet a Marine, Jon had been given a set of keys to the executive suite. Jon was told explicitly how to behave if he wanted to grow as a Marine. What strikes me about this list is how many of the items are behaviors. A US Marine behaves dependably, decisively, with integrity, unselfishly, and courageously. These behaviors transcend the battlefield and the warrior spirit that is so important to the Marine Corps. They translate into personal behaviors, so becoming a Marine becomes a lifelong engagement. Once a Marine, always a Marine. I have heard people who had not worn their uniforms in twenty years recite verbatim every one of these key behaviors. While it would be strikingly shortsighted to say this list of leadership behaviors is solely responsible for the excellence of the US Marine Corps, they do lay an important foundation.

Summary

Rules, routines, and behaviors make up the sequence of the genetic code for a system of organizational leadership. They join people, money, and knowledge to the larger purpose of leadership.

One of the case studies in *An Everyone Culture* is Next Jump, a $2 billion (2016) e-commerce company that wants to revolutionize workplace culture. Next Jump has a focus of "self-development above all else." Self-development includes an emphasis on behavior, character formation, and leadership development. Next Jump understands that character is like a muscle. It can be developed with exercise. Next Jump also believes there is a clear connection between character and business growth. What it calls "character imbalances," such as too much confidence or too much humility, can lead to paralysis. The authors explain, "The growth in the company's leadership took off as leaders discovered and consistently practiced the development of character as a muscle that could be exercised, helping people become more humble or more confident."[33]

Behavior (and yes, I am equating behavior with character) is important. These highly successful organizations recognize behavior, character, and conduct in the workplace are clearly connected to growth, profitably, and value creation. Improving manager and leader behavior and character is no longer the exclusive domain of personal morality, and therefore, nobody's business. It is a conversation that, in today's economy, is vital for a strong employee experience and creating maximum value for patients/customers.

Leadership Debrief and Exercises

What Erin did at a neighborhood elementary school is a model for any organization that strives for excellence and exceptional performance.

Start the following exercise alone, then repeat it with your team.

1. Identify eight to ten critical behaviors that support your primary purpose as a leader or your organizational core values. Write each one on a card or Post-it-note. Let them sit on your desk for a few days as you reflect on your own behavior around the office.

2. Now the hard part—score yourself for each behavior with ten being really good and one being awful.

33 Kegan, Robert and Lisa Laskow Lahey. An Everyone Culture: Becoming a Deliberately Developmental Organization. Harvard Business Review Press. Kindle Edition, 2016. p. 135-6.

3. Look at each behavior and define it. What does it feel like to you when you exercise each behavior? What do you think it feels like for your team when you demonstrate each behavior?

_____

_____

_____

_____

_____

_____

_____

_____

_____

_____

4. Repeat this exercise with your staff: create a set of behaviors, define each one, but do it collaboratively. Let them own the behaviors. This will enhance your ability to manage.

5. Write the set of core rules, routines, and behaviors into a team charter.

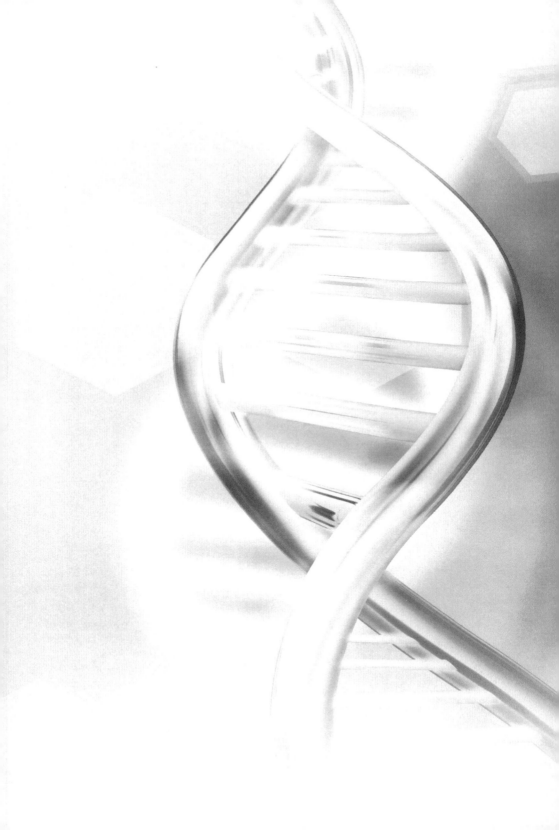

SECTION 4
MEASURING SYSTEM PERFORMANCE

"If you cannot measure it, you cannot improve it."

— Lord Kelvin

As you are reading these pages, your renal-endocrine system is regulating your blood pressure to ensure blood flow to vital tissues and organs. At the same time, enzymes are unzipping your strands of DNA in a process of replication. Other enzymes take the two halves and create two new strands. All the while, the cell is monitoring the process. In the rare event that the molecule is damaged, the cell will send in a repair team to fix the damage. This is a grossly simplified way of explaining how the human body monitors its systems to ensure all are operating according to requirements. It also illustrates one of the central attributes of a system—they are self-monitoring.

In Chapter 5, I referenced a catastrophic system failure when a neurological clinic changed the purpose of its system from patient safety to revenue generation. Physicians and nurses alike filed forty-nine complaints against the new director accusing him of dangerous and unprofessional behavior. He and the leadership team saw this as disgruntled employees resisting change. From a systems perspective, this was simply the system responding to a perceived threat. What I discovered in my research is that high-performing organizations, teams, and individual leaders always have a way of measuring the effectiveness of their leadership systems. It could be formal or informal, but there is always a way. And it always includes a strong emphasis on measuring the experience of the workforce.

***

On September 15, 1924, citizens of Abilene, Texas, realized a much-needed dream. West Texas Baptist Sanitarium, a Christian hospital, opened its doors to help the sick and suffering of the Texas Midwest. As the name implies, the hospital was a Baptist institution, and it took its Christian mission seriously. West Texas Baptist soon ran into hard times when the stock market crashed in 1929, launching the Great Depression. Unemployment mushroomed in West Texas, but people still got sick and needed healthcare. The community wanted a hospital, and they rallied. The Hendricks, a married couple, made a major financial gift to pay off debts and expand the hospital. In gratitude, the hospital still carries their name—Hendrick Health System.

Ninety-four years later, Hendrick Health System operates a 564-bed hospital and a family of services that includes a women's center, rehabilitation hospital, cancer center, hospice center, NICU, and other services. Hendrick draws its patients from Abilene and nineteen surrounding counties and enjoys an enviable reputation. Surveys find that 64 percent of the citizens say they prefer Hendrick. Though still part of the Texas Baptist General Conference network of healthcare systems, Hendrick makes no distinction about who it serves. Patients come from all walks of life, regardless of their ability to pay. Outside of the board of directors, who are members of the Texas Baptist Convention, the 3,000 people who work there represent diverse cultures, faiths, and languages.

Until his retirement in 2018, Tim Lancaster was Hendrick's long-time president and chief executive officer. Hendrick has a habit of hanging on to its CEOs. The average tenure has been twenty-three-and-a-half years, while the average tenure elsewhere for healthcare CEOs is three to five years. Friends from the area tell me Hendrick has a tradition of growing its own leadership and then keeping them around for as long as possible.

Hendrick has another notable achievement. For fourteen consecutive years, it has been recognized by Gallup with the Great Workplace Award. It is one of only three organizations in the Gallup database with this level of performance and the only healthcare organization. This award is how Hendrick measures its leadership system.

In my interview, I asked Tim how Hendrick was able to achieve this level of performance.

He patiently said, "Well, we emphasize it."

As it turns out, he was not kidding. During my conversation, it struck me that he liked the kind of math John Heer and Captain David Marquet had used. Like them, he chose to have 3,000 passionately engaged healthcare providers, who are giving their absolute best to their patients and community, over one person telling 2,999 others what to do. Hendrick takes leadership seriously, so seriously that each leader has their personal leadership evaluated by their subordinates and ranked against the universe of Gallup engagement scores. The objective is for each work unit to be in the top 75 percent of those actively engaged as measured by Gallup. If a leader or manager's workforce falls into the bottom 25 percent, it triggers a formal assessment. It could be the organization, the manager, or a combination of both. But if it is the manager, they will probably be reassigned, if they have not already reassigned themselves.

At Hendrick, leadership is important, and they seem to have realized that the connection to an engaged workforce is the relationship between leader and staff. For those of us not in healthcare, this might seem a little harsh or intrusive. However, it turns out that the single greatest determinate in hospital mortality is the nurses' level of engagement. At Hendrick, leadership is not left up to personal style, value, or goodwill. An engaged workforce is a matter of life and death. Therefore, they have designed a leadership system that will actively engage the workforce. But I think there is more. This next chapter will illustrate how organizations like Hendrick have made engagement a central fixture of their business strategy, and they treat it like a precondition for their strategic success.

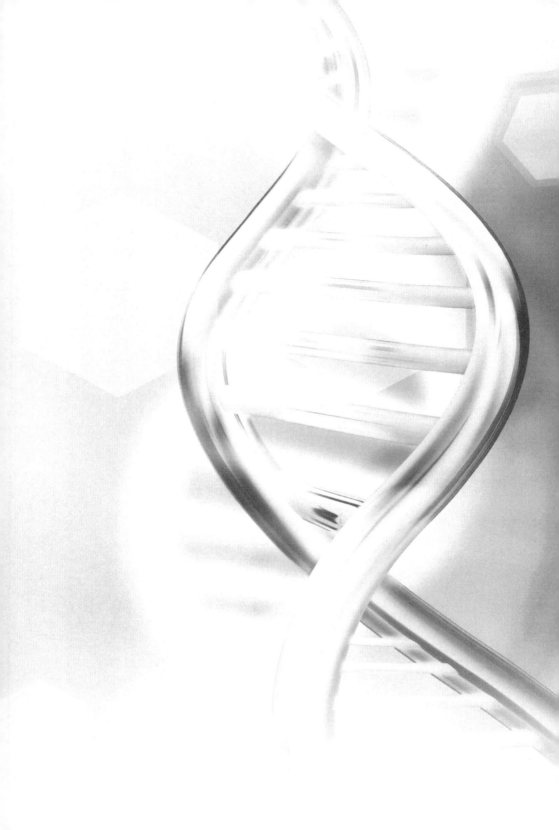

CHAPTER 12

LEVERAGING ENGAGEMENT AS STRATEGY

"Always treat your employees exactly as you
want them to treat your best customers."

— Stephen R. Covey

In January 1982, Dennis Bakke and Roger Sant incorporated AES (Applied Energy Services) with a $60,000 bank loan and $1 million of capital raised from family and friends. The objective was to create a business that reduced the cost of electrical power. But another part of their company made it a top case study in elite business schools. They wanted to make AES a fun place to work. Not the Friday night pizza party kind of fun, but the kind of fun where the workforce enjoys going to work, finds value and significance in their work, understands how their job contributes to the overall mission, and also earns a livable wage anywhere in the world.

The company grew quickly. By 2000, AES was a global energy company with operations in thirty-one countries, 40,000 employees, and nearly $34 billion in assets. That same year, ING Barings named Dennis Bakke CEO of the year.

In his book *Joy at Work*, Bakke recounts the story of one Christmas party he attended for staff operating an energy plant near Mystic, Connecticut. During the evening, the plant manager asked members of various task forces to stand and be recognized for their contributions to operations. At Bakke's table, a man stood and was recognized for his contribution to the budgeting task force, which set the operating budget for the entire plant. Later, Eileen, Bakke's wife, asked the man where he worked in the plant. She assumed he was a senior financial manager or analyst developing detailed corporate budgets.

His response, "I'm a security guard."[34]

I suspect when Bakke and Sant incorporated AES, they were thinking of an engaged workforce as a moral imperative. It was morally appropriate to pay every worker a livable wage, whether they lived in Connecticut, Africa, or Latin America. However, what I see is that they created a business strategy that required a fully engaged workforce. Paying people a livable wage no matter where they lived may have been a moral value (which can easily be ignored), but they coded it into their operation's DNA when they made it a strategic imperative.

We know a highly engaged workforce creates value. The good news is more organizations are beginning to understand this. The latest Gallup poll reveal the number of actively engaged workers is on the rise. The 2019 numbers show that 35 percent of the American workforce is actively engaged or takes psychological ownership of their organizations. This is a record high.

There is more good news. The number of actively disengaged, those who are actively sabotaging their employers, has dropped from 16 to 13 percent. This, too, is a record, a record low for two consecutive years. However, it still leaves 52 percent of the workplace unengaged. They go to work, collect a paycheck, and contribute little to innovation or customer value. They do what they are told and little else. They are also looking for another job.[35]

---

34 Bakke, Dennis. *Joy at Work*. Seattle, WA: Dennis Bakke, 2005. p. 106
35 Hunter, Jim. "4 Factors Driving Record-High Employee Engagement in U.S." Gallup, Inc. February 4, 2020.

Another Gallup report details specifically the kind of value an engaged workforce creates. In the report, "Building a High-Development Culture Through Your Employee Engagement Strategy,"[36] an engaged workforce results in:

- 41 percent lower absenteeism
- 58 percent fewer patient safety incidents (healthcare application)
- 24 percent less turnover in high-turnover organizations
- 59 percent less turnover in low-turnover organizations
- 28 percent less shrinkage
- 70 percent fewer safety incidents
- 40 percent fewer quality defects
- 10 percent higher customer ratings
- 17 percent higher productivity
- 20 percent higher sales
- 21 percent higher profitability

The astounding thing is that an engaged workforce does not cost a penny more than a non-engaged workforce. In fact, it's cheaper. Everybody who walks in the door comes with a complete set of human DNA that abounds with creativity, innovation, and passion. The challenge is how to unleash it. How do we free it from the shackles of corporate and human fear and intimidation? Moving the dial on the 52 percent who go to work without passion, without engaging their innate creativity, and without full mental and emotional engagement represents the potential for the single biggest boost to a national economy. We have seen the scientific age, the industrial revolution, and the

36 Gallup, Inc. "Building a High-Development Culture Through Your Employee Engagement Strategy." 2019. p. 5.

knowledge economy. Could we be looking at the next new wave of opportunity—the engagement revolution? I hope so.

Reading popular literature on workforce engagement suggests the minds, hearts, passions, and creativity of the workforce can be bought with money and trinkets or coerced through discipline. Except there is not a shred of evidence that any of this works long-term. The same Gallup article makes it clear that engagement comes down to leadership and the relationship between manager and subordinates. High-performing organizations hold management accountable and change the way they lead. To do this across the enterprise takes more than syrupy slogans, inspirational emails, and visually engaging websites. It requires an enterprise-wide approach to leadership that recognizes the workforce as human beings who carry with them limitless potential and opportunity. Treat them well and they will gladly repay in kind.

However, leadership cannot be divorced from strategy. A leader's primary responsibility is to execute strategy. When workforce engagement becomes a strategic imperative or a central component of competitive advantage, leadership systems will be designed to reward leaders for their workforce's level of engagement. The following stories will show how three elite organizations integrated their engagement strategies with their business strategies.

***

Car dealerships rank last in organizations we trust. So, when a car dealership is recognized with the nation's highest award for excellence, it is worth noting and asking how.

In 1995, Don Chalmers moved his family to Albuquerque, New Mexico, and opened a Ford dealership. He had a rather old-fashioned business model in mind—provide customers with real value, treat them well, and treat the workforce like he wanted them to treat customers. His motto was *"Real value, real people, real simple."* Starting out, he broke quickly from tradition and hired people without experience in selling cars. Too many experienced salespeople had to be retrained to think of the customer first.

Don also personally took on the principles of servant leadership and expected the same for each leader and manager. Since its inception, Don Chalmers Ford has received Ford's President's Award, Ford's highest award for dealership excellence, fourteen times. In 2016, it was recognized with the nation's highest award for excellence, the highly coveted Malcolm Baldrige National Quality Award. In the Albuquerque market, it consistently outranks Toyota and Honda in customer satisfaction scores. Its sales volume and profitability rank with the industry's best.

Despite Don's death in 2014, his dealership has continued with his values, systems, and ethics. There has been no drop in performance—evidence that he left behind a leadership system that could continue without him.

But something else is unusual about Don Chalmers Ford. It is closed on one of the most important car-buying days of the week: Sunday. Don felt Sunday was a family day, and he wanted his staff and their families to be together on Sundays. As of 2016, the company's workforce retention was 87 percent. In 2015 and 2016, out of 5,000 Ford dealerships, it was rated the best to work for.

In reading the dealership's 2016 Malcolm Baldrige National Quality Award Application, I was struck by two things: 1) Don Chalmers made servant leadership the path to creating an engaged workforce (the two sides of his double helix), and 2) Don Chalmers made an engaged workforce a central fixture in his business strategy. While it may have started out as a moral consideration, I think it became a requirement for Don Chalmers Ford's strategic success. When an organization becomes the number-one dealership to work for in a universe of 5,000 dealerships, engagement is more than morality. It is a strategic pathway to success. Their 2016 Baldrige application said, "Comprehensive and critical workforce engagement...is at the core of DCF's (Don Chalmers Ford) integrated strategic planning system."[37]

***

I am struck by the similarities between Jeff Kaas and Don Chalmers. Both are men of faith who seem to be guided by their faith. Both take the responsibility of caring for their workers seriously. Both have adopted the principles of servant leadership as one side of their double helix and engaging the workforce as the other side. Both contribute significantly to their respective communities. As I am writing this, we are at the apex of the COVID-19 virus pandemic. There are major shortages of basic protective equipment for healthcare workers. Kaas Tailored was one of the first manufacturing companies in America to voluntarily shift its production to making personal protection equipment. Their challenge: 100 million face masks and shields.

I am also struck by similarities in their business strategies. Value. Chalmers Ford wants to deliver maximum value to its customers. This begins with a highly engaged workforce, who then deliver this value. Because Kaas Tailored is a manufacturing company, value is different, but the goal is the same. A central feature of this business strate-

---

37 2016 National Malcolm Baldrige National Quality Award application. p. 7.

gy is eliminating waste in its manufacturing processes. The company might be guilty of making it an obsession, but this strategy would be impossible without a highly engaged workforce. Kaas workers find and eliminate waste. Their leaders and managers are trained to mentor and coach them in the quest to eradicate waste. As I stated earlier, 200 employees initiate 1,000-1,250 *kaizen* initiatives each year. This means that, on average, each employee is finding five or six opportunities to eliminate waste and improve basic operational processes every year, and each one saves the company $1,000 a year.

This is one way to measure workforce engagement. But there is another—it is certainly a more subjective way, but it is indicative of their culture. I noticed it before I ever walked into their facilities. I had arrived at Kaas Tailored to begin my tour about twenty minutes early. As I was sitting in my car, sipping my morning latte, I was struck by something unusual. Everyone I saw entering the building was smiling. They looked happy going to work. Then, on the tour, everyone I met seemed to take pride in their work, and it was obvious they were engaged. When I walked by, they would look at me, make eye contact, and smile. In twenty-five years of consulting, I have walked into hundreds of organizations, and I have never seen a workforce that looked that happy.

How serious does Jeff Kaas take his servant leadership? I interviewed him after my tour. When I asked how he might measure his leadership system, he said, "I don't know, but I think it will be the number of employees we can get trained and then move to other firms that can pay them more."

True to Jeff's system of servant leadership, he is thinking of his staff and how *he* can serve *them*. Many of his workers are new to America, so finding well-paying manufacturing jobs is key to their assimilation into American culture and its opportunities.

∗∗∗

When Paul O'Neil took over as CEO of Alcoa, his vision was of a workplace free of accidents. Not almost free, but zero workplace accidents. This is an audacious objective in such a dangerous workplace environment. From my research about Paul O'Neil, he considered an accident-free workplace a moral imperative. He has frequently said that no one should ever be afraid for their safety when going to work. However, to create such a safe workplace in an industrial environment without a highly engaged workforce would be impossible. When Paul passed out his personal phone number and said, "Call me if your supervisor does not listen when you have an idea about improving your safety." Every leader, manager, and production lead was put on notice. A workforce engaged to eliminate accidents just became a strategic priority.

Safety is critical, and the path to getting there is to get every eye available on this singular objective. When safety is the lens through which every system, process, and procedure is measured, quality is increased, and value is created; then safety and engagement become more than an ethic or value—they become strategic. When the safety report is the first report at every board and management meeting, safety and its requirement for engagement becomes strategic. When profit and shareholder value become dependent upon safety, and the path to safety is an engaged workforce, then engagement becomes strategic and needs to be measured and monitored as such. Paul made that happen in the workplace. The evidence suggests his successors are following the example.

Summary

Over my career, I have facilitated strategic planning sessions with clients, I have been a participant in strategic planning initiatives, and I have taught strategic planning. I hold a professional certification in strategic planning. One of the nasty little secrets about strategic plans is that most of them end up as pretty documents on a table by the reception desk, and about six months later, they go into storage.

While researching and writing this book, an observation struck me several times: What level of workforce engagement is required to execute strategy? In retrospect, I think every strategy session I have ever been involved with was missing a component, and that component is the level of workforce engagement required to execute the plan. Occasionally in these strategy sessions, we have discussed workforce capabilities and capacities. However, I never remember a discussion about a level of workforce engagement necessary to execute strategy. There has always been an assumption that the workforce would happily get on board with this exciting new strategy. In retrospect, these assumptions are grossly unrealistic. How realistic is a strategy when only 35 percent of the workforce is engaged with it, and 13 percent are actively sabotaging the organization and its strategy?

What I learned from organizations like AES, Chalmers Ford, Erin at the elementary school, and Captain Marquet of the USS Santa Fe is that each of them aligned the requirement for an engaged workforce with their business strategy. Chalmers Ford recognized a connection between the level of engagement of their workforce, and the value they could deliver to their customers. Kaas Tailored determined that its strategy of eliminating waste required a fully engaged workforce. Furthermore, Paul O'Neil figured out that his mission to produce an industrial workplace with zero accidents required a workforce that was totally engaged with this vision. The math would not work if the only people looking for opportunities to make the workplace safer were managers. Paul needed every set of eyes available focused on his vision of a workplace with zero accidents and injuries.

There are two lessons here:

1. When workforce engagement rises to the level of a strategic requirement, then individual leaders take the engagement of their staff seriously.

2. To engage the entire workforce requires a leadership system that trains every leader and manager to coach and mentor, rather than control and demand.

Leadership Debrief and Exercises

Now is a good time to review your strategic objectives. Write out the basic parts in bullet points. If you have short- and long-term objectives, list them in order.

For each one, write a brief statement about how the level of workforce engagement will impact progress toward each objective.

1. _____

_____

_____

_____

_____

2. _____
_____
_____
_____
_____

3. _____
_____
_____
_____
_____

If you are going through this exercise with your leadership team, have each member write out the statements individually. Then share your statements openly and honestly.

Now try this: Ask a group of your midlevel and emerging managers/ leaders to do the same. What differences or similarities in perspective do you see?

Finally, look at your engagement data and identify any gaps. If you don't have any data on the level of workforce engagement, estimate it. Then cut that amount in half. Every time I have asked the leadership team about engagement levels, they inevitably rave about how committed their workforce is. Then I talk to the workforce and it is pretty clear huge gaps exist between the perspectives of senior leaders and front line workers.

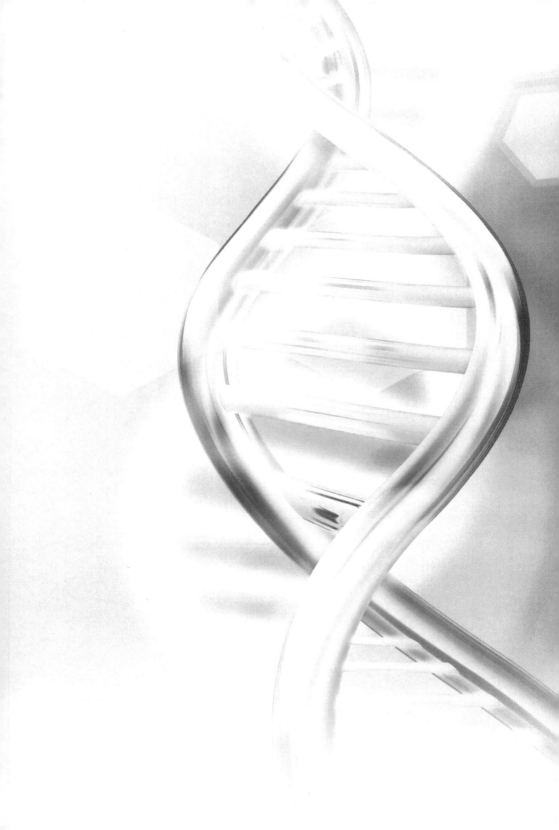

CHAPTER 13

LEVERAGING THE POWER OF DESIGN

"The best way to predict your future is to create it."

— Peter Drucker

You have seen that there are three parts to a leadership system: the purpose, the resources, and the interactions—how those resources interact to create the purpose. Now you want to start your own journey and develop your own leadership system. I will walk you through how one rural hospital did this. If you are a team leader, the process would be identical.

Mason General Hospital and Family of Clinics is a small rural hospital that also owns and operates ten primary and specialty clinics. It is a challenging community. Shelton has been a logging town, and with logging restrictions, the economy has shrunk. The results are high rates of unemployment, drug and alcohol abuse, and consequently, a higher than normal volume of patients seeking care in Mason's emergency department. This is not a place where graduates of elite medical schools like Harvard and Stanford go when large urban healthcare centers are making attractive offers and offering signing bonuses. However, just because Mason is small, does not mean it can be complaisant about the quality of care. It is owned and operated by the community. Its board of supervisors are elected officials, so if quality of care lags, the supervisors will hear about it from their neighbors. Furthermore, when doc-

tors and nurses walk into a grocery store, it's highly probable that patients will recognize them by name. The very size of Mason means it is
an integral part of the community, with high accountability.

In addition, several large healthcare systems are "circling overhead,"
waiting to acquire Mason at the first sign of trouble. While losing its
independence might be good economics for the acquiring company,
it would be disastrous for the community. Its long-term strategy is to
create an exceptionally healthy community, which will require it to be
fully integrated with the network of social service organizations serving the community. This means partnering transparently with first re-
sponders, social and mental health services, and larger hospitals in the
area, even though they might also be competitors.

Eric Moll, CEO of Mason General Hospital and Family of Clinics, is a
thoughtful and caring leader. He attended elite schools but has chosen
to live and work in this community. I was privileged to work with him
and his staff in their initial journey into the Baldrige Quality Framework, so I was thrilled when he asked if I could help him design a
formal model of leadership. He wanted an approach to leadership for
the whole organization, consistently deployed, and measurable. My
partner and I saw this as an opportunity to design a leadership system
from the ground up. As such, our first task was to identify what the
system was going to produce—its purpose.

Our first meeting included the senior executive team: Eric, Eileen
the chief operating officer (COO), and Rick the chief financial officer
(CFO). Our initial objective was to identify the system's purpose or
output. After clarification and some discussion, Rick suggested exceptional health as the primary purpose or output of their leadership
system, which aligned with the hospital's vision statement of "United
Community, Empowered People, Exceptional Health."

As the discussion continued, Eileen was quiet and thoughtful. I finally asked her what she was thinking. Her response was classic. She noted that a leadership system must produce staff who feel empowered. Only empowered staff will take that extra step or make that extra phone call that will deliver exceptional health. "Patients also need to feel a sense of empowerment about their own healthcare. We do not deliver healthcare to them. We deliver healthcare with them." Since Mason is a community-owned hospital, Eileen felt their community needed a sense of empowerment, of real partnership, working together in the delivery of exceptional healthcare for the community. In her usual wisdom, Eileen had articulated the most powerful, but least obvious, part of a system—the purpose.

When I walked out of Eric's office, I was sure our meeting had been the most important of my twenty-five years of consulting. As my partner and I walked out the front door of the hospital, we looked at each other and simultaneously said, "What just happened in there?"

Eric, Rick, and Eileen also realized the potential of what we had just discussed. They saw the opportunity of every leader and manager rowing to the same cadence, one that could catapult them forward in their mission and vision.

They also realized something else. Not every leader and manager would be able to function in a way that would generate an empowered workforce, and others would need time to make the transition. Wisely, they set up a process where designing the system would take nine months and implementation would take another year.

With the central purpose identified, multiple workshops to identify the remaining components of the system followed: system behaviors, routines, and key metrics that would determine system effectiveness. They were already doing significant work developing their workforce, they were implementing Lean throughout their system, and they had designed processes that built innovation into their daily work, so we did not feel we needed to address these key resources further. Toward the end of these workshops, Melissa, the chief nursing officer (CNO), sat back in her chair and studied the graphics that had been developed and displayed on a wall. Then she said, "I have always been promoted because I was a good nurse; then they put this leadership tag on me, but I did not have a clue what I was supposed to do. Now I know."

How to Design a System of Leadership

Not too many organizations have intentionally designed a leadership system. Most who have don't really understand what they have done. Mason General Hospital is one of the few that has intentionally designed a system of leadership from the ground up. John Heer at North Mississippi Health Services is another. I think Captain David Marquet of the *USS Santa Fe* did it, as did Erin the elementary school principal. Most organizations just allow their leadership system to evolve over time until it looks like a house where the homeowner has not made basic maintenance a priority. The roof sags, settling foundations result in cracks in the walls, siding is missing, and plastic covers a few windows. Yet, somehow, people still live there.

In designing a leadership system, one thing should be kept in mind. Some will embrace it and the process; others will not. Those who are intent on doing leadership their way will probably walk out. Others will need to be encouraged to move on. The goal is to minimize the disruption while maintaining the integrity of the objective, which is long-term sustainability. When I ask Rhonda Stewart, the Transformational Sensei and my tour guide at Virginia Mason Hospital, how traditional leaders handled the hospital's requirements, she said, "Many who are hired from the outside don't make it and move on." That was one reason Virginia Mason works to develop its leaders internally.

Here is a step-by-step process that should result in a well-designed leadership system and cause the least disruption.

With the Executive Team

Step 1. Gather your executive team and begin discussing the purpose and end results of organizational leadership. Ask them to put their ideas on note cards. I suggest you use 5" x 6" cards, one idea per card, and then post them on a board or wall. The goal is to get these ideas down to one or two words and ensure they reflect the employee experience. They can also reflect the experience of other stakeholders, but they *must* reflect the experience of the workforce. If you can do this in one meeting, great, but it might take several. That is okay.

With Senior Leadership (The Broader Group of Leaders)

Step 2A. Identify behaviors critical to your purpose or output. This process is similar to Step 1. Give everyone plenty of 5" x 6" cards and have them write down one idea per card. Only this time, you are looking for specific behaviors that will support your purpose. These will sound a lot like values, but make them action-oriented. Examples: Behave with integrity, treat staff with respect, and give credit to the team. You will be looking for eight to ten behaviors.

Step 2B. Assign a team to define in detail what each behavior means. For example, what does it look like when a leader leads in a trustworthy manner? The language should reflect both feelings and actions, such as, "A leader building trust will make their team feel they can rely on their supervisor." Don't expect to do this in a meeting or two. It will take time. This is where collaboration comes in. Give it time to develop.

Step 3A. Design your rules. Every organization has them, written and unwritten. Identifying important rules is a twostep process: 1) Identify existing rules, and 2) eliminate outdated rules and write new ones. Again, give everyone in senior leadership 5" x 6" cards. Everyone should write three to five rules, one rule per card. Post them on a whiteboard or in another place where everyone can see them. Eliminate duplicates. Ask if there are more rules. Just seeing them go up on a wall should trigger additional ideas. Keep doing this until there is no further conversation.

Step 3B. Identify the rules that support your purpose and those that do not. Some will be natural; that is okay. Acknowledge that some rules are counter to a culture of collaboration. This needs to be a very frank and transparent discussion. Does collaboration mean it is acceptable for a leader to take the credit for success and put blame on their team when failure occurs? You might even consider ceremoniously burning rules that need to be broken. Take the cards and burn them.

Step 3C. Write your new set of rules. For example, if your purpose is to create a culture of collaboration, you may want to discuss an open-door policy. Or should there even be offices? Maybe an open office design is better suited for collaboration. Discuss meeting rules. Does a seating arrangement make a difference? (It usually does.) If collaboration is the purpose of leadership, there will need to be rules about listening. You will not accomplish this task in one meeting. Give it time.

Step 4A. Design your routines. The process is the same as in Step 3. Identify those routines that do not support a culture of collaboration.

One observation could be there are no routines at all. This is perfectly acceptable.

Step 4B. *Identify routines that do support a culture of collaboration.* These may need to be organizational or team specific. Leaders of a marketing team may have different routines than, say, a leader of a manufacturing team, or the purchasing team. In the Lean world, routines can be likened to standard daily, weekly, or monthly work. However, no matter which team, you will probably find broadly defined routines. For example, some organizations may have a weekly routine called a huddle where the senior executives review progress toward strategic initiatives. Other organizations may require a daily huddle to review operational requirements for the day. Other routines would be a daily genba or a time when the leader will be out of their office and visiting with teams. Each team should have three to five routines designed for them that every leader will follow. This creates institutional muscle memory, so don't expect it to happen overnight.

Step 5. Put the above into a Leadership Charter. Ideally, a Leadership Charter is a one-page document that can be turned into a poster or quickly referenced. Provide background data on a separate document. For example, the definitions of acceptable behaviors might need to be in a separate document.

Step 6. Measurement and monitoring. Every system can be measured and monitored. Most are self-monitoring. Once you get your system going, the good news is that it will be self-sustaining, and this produces long-term sustainability. Twelve years after Paul O'Neil retired from Aloca, they were still improving their safety records. How? Because he left in place systems to improve safety. Within each leadership system, there are one to three ways of measuring effectiveness. This is the place where less is more and simple is better than complex.

Use the same process as before—5" x 6" cards; everybody writes down three to five ways of measuring the system. These should be measures tied directly back to the purpose. If the purpose is collaboration, you are looking for how to measure levels of collaboration. If the purpose is empowerment, how will you measure an empowered workforce? In other words, do *not* use market share or ROI if your purpose is collaboration.

Ultimately, at some level, you are measuring workforce engagement. However, what is even more important is that you are measuring leadership from the workforce's perspective. Several independent surveys can measure this for you. However, there may be other ways to measure the system. Here are a few to consider:

- Workforce safety
- Patient safety (healthcare)
- Fear in the workplace
- 360-degree performance reviews
- Turnover
- Number of days lost due to workplace injuries

You have just completed the first phase in designing a leadership system. The second phase will take longer, but it will eventually need to be incorporated into the rules, routines, and behaviors listed above. This is a recurring process, so don't expect to get it right the first time. From my research, the highest-performing organizations review, assess, and improve their leadership systems continually. Erin's staff reviewed their charter annually and made adjustments. New teachers brought new perspectives so the process kept their charter fresh and vibrant.

Now repeat the exercise with your team. Do not share your responses with them until maybe at the end.

Have fun.

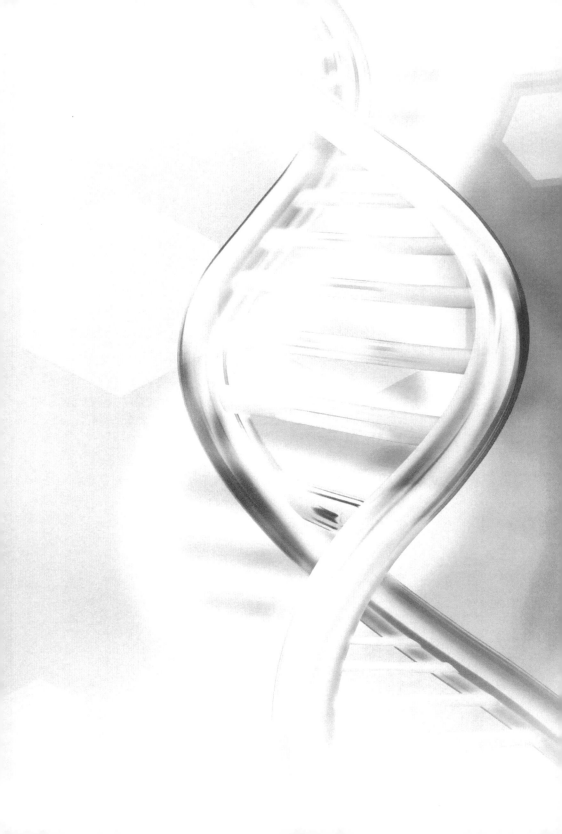

CREATING THE SUSTAINABLE FUTURE

"An important function of almost every system
is to ensure its own perpetuation."

— Donella H. Meadows, *Thinking in Systems: A Primer*

When Paul O'Neil left Alcoa in 2000, the company had 140,000 employees spread across thirty-six countries. It was safer to work in an Alcoa smelter turning 2,000° (F) liquid aluminum into soda cans than the back office of an insurance company shuffling paper. When Paul took over in 1987, there were 1.86 lost workday incidents per 100 employees per year. When he left, it was down to 0.2. Two years after he retired, the number was down to 0.05 lost workday incidents per 100 employees.[38] The lesson here is that one of the key attributes of a system is that it is self-sustaining unless changed by an external force. In the same way, mediocre organizations tend to stay that way unless an external force moves them. That force can be a dynamic new leader. However, when that leader moves on, if they have not made any systemic change, the organization will revert back to...average.

In twenty-five years of consulting, I have never met anyone who was excited to work for an organization that was...average. However, I have met hundreds who would willingly sacrifice personal time to improve their organizations and be part of a championship-caliber

38 Lagace, Martha. *HBS Working Knowledge.* Nov. 2002.

team. My objective in writing this book has been to give a voice to the millions of workers who want to work for an organization of high performance and excellence. Frankly, this group, over half the working population, represents a massive untapped resource. However, to tap this resource, to realize the opportunity it represents, will require systems of organizational leadership that are designed to unleash the basic human capacity for innovation, creativity, and sacrifice. Relying on the generous goodwill of dynamic individuals is too risky.

What Are You Going to Do?

As I finish the final editing of this manuscript, we are battling the COVID-19 pandemic. Unemployment in the US is nearly 15 percent, the highest since the Great Depression of 1929. Millions of workers are working remotely from their homes. School students are learning remotely, and video conferencing has replaced face-to-face meetings. Google, Facebook, and other large tech companies are giving their staffs the option to work from home for the next six months.

Additionally, another trend will only speed up. A 2015 article, published by Forbes, documents that contract workers comprise 40 percent of the US workforce. In general, these workers enjoy significantly fewer rights than traditional employees. They can be told at 5:00 p.m. on a Friday night that they have just worked their last day and be shown the door. If the contract employee was hired through a third party, the contracting agency may be told on Friday at 5:00, "Tell Jim not to show up on Monday; we are done with him."

I will not pretend to be a futurist, but I think the trends for more remote workers and contract workers is set. Google now employs more contract workers than traditional employees. These trends will require innovating the foundations of leadership. When workers can work from wherever they want, their leaders lose a lot of control. The requirement for trust will need to replace the requirement for control. Organizational power will be transferred to the worker who can control where and when they work. Collaboration will look different. Virtual meeting technology, while providing the mechanism for collaboration, cannot create a culture of collaboration. Individual leaders will need to learn to lead differently.

This is also true for leading contract workers. I will resist the temptation to write about the morality of contract workers being treated as second-class corporate citizens. From the standpoint of leadership, the challenge is the same with the traditional employee—how to engage them so you can capture their full intellectual and emotional capacity. Forty percent of the workforce being contracted represents massive intellectual capital that is being ignored when it could be tapped and mined for the same cost.

All of this convinces me that now is the time to understand leadership as an organizational system. Systems can be designed to requirements and specifications to capture the full opportunity of millennials who represent the most highly education generation in history. This includes systems that can be designed to keep remote and contract workers engaged. If I have convinced you that organizational leadership can be understood as a system that can be designed to a specific DNA, it is your turn to take that understanding and act upon it. I have a basic bent toward action. Talk is cheap, and there is way too much of it in my opinion. So here is my challenge to you:

1. Within the next thirty days, gather your leadership team and have a frank conversation about what the workforce needs to fully engage with the organization. Focus on the workers' experience. If

you hire contract workers, do *not* exclude them. The experience of the workforce is what will get passed on to your customers, so this conversation is vital because it has clear economic and competitive impacts. Then ask them, either through personal interviews or through an anonymous survey, what they want to experience. The goal is to learn the difference between what you think your leadership is like and what it is really like.

2.   Then, with the data in mind, select a singular purpose—a description of what leadership should produce to engage the workforce. Someone on the team will argue that the purpose of leadership is to "get results." True, but what kinds of results and how? Results are the byproduct of workers. The objective is language that will capture the purpose from the workforce's perspective. Be prepared for things like safety, relationship, respect, collaboration, and ownership. These are all transcendent values, and from my research, this is what your workforce is looking for. Economic results get boring and flow to shareholders anyway, bypassing the workers.

3.   Now put the pride away and start building the system.

   A.   Develop the Leadership Charter.

   B.   Determine how the leadership system will be measured and monitored.

   C.   Discuss if you want to be a DDO (Deliberately Developmental Organization). What would be the implications? If you don't want to be a DDO, be honest and just say "no." However, if you do, then you need a clear approach to development that will align with the Charter.

      a.   How will you develop your emerging leaders and the general workforce?

b. How will you develop your approach to eliminating waste?

c. How will you create a culture of everyday innovation?

Summary

Discussions of leadership go back at least as far as Aristotle. Most of what we know about modern management theory has been in place since Henry Ford was pushing Model Ts out of his first assembly line in Highland Park, Michigan. It is time to reengineer the DNA of organizational leadership.

Today's workforce represents the most highly educated workforce to ever grace the planet. Yet we are obsessed with this leader-follower mentality that says the leader commands and controls the followers. This makes the current workforce a massively untapped resource. As George Clifton, chair of the Gallup organization, said, "The American leadership philosophy simply doesn't work anymore." Furthermore, millennials, who are flooding the workplace, are not interested in being led. To capture the full opportunity for sustainable excellence and performance requires designed leadership systems and then training and coaching each leader to its requirements. This is the only way the math works. Relying on a cult of personality just does not work. The math only works if *all* leaders are trained to the system's requirements.

My Desire for You

In twelve years, John Wooden coached the UCLA Bruins basketball team to ten national championships and four perfect 30-0 seasons, including eighty-eight consecutive victories. Few expect this record will ever be broken. By today's standards, Wooden was a relic. He abhorred profanity in favor of poetry and seldom talked about winning. But he was a master at system design, and his system built the greatest teams in the history of collegiate basketball. Then he trained every player to the requirements of his system and never wavered. Captain David Marquet did the same thing with the USS Santa Fe. He designed a system of leadership and then trained every officer to its requirements. Erin did the same thing at her elementary school, and the Southcentral Foundation did the same thing in Anchorage, Alaska. Paul O'Neil did the same thing at Alcoa, as did Jeff Kaas at Kaas Tailored.

I am absolutely convinced that this kind of elite performance is available to anyone who wants to put it to work. I'm not saying it is easy. If your organization is average, and assuming it has 100 leaders, I am confident most of them will feel leadership is a personal style, and they may walk at the idea of a designed system that will instruct them on how to lead. However, those who stay, and those who come after them, will be given the opportunity to work for an organization that rises to the top, long-term. What is more, you will be giving your entire workforce the opportunity to be part of a championship-caliber team, not just occasionally, but year after year.

I started out my introduction by telling you the story of my son and a group of middle school boys who wanted to play basketball for their little private school that could barely field a team. In three years, this group of boys went from winless, to an undefeated championship season. They had no superstar talent, but they had a coach who designed a system for how to play the game of basketball as a team. Win or lose, they would play as a team. Furthermore, Coach Will loved those boys enough to care about them as boys who would someday turn into young men. The result was they flourished on the basketball court. And now, years later, I am watching them flourish as young men and husbands. Will's system is doing what every system does: it replicates.

My challenge to you is to think about your team or your organization. What kind of leadership system will give your workforce the thrill of being on a championship team? But also, will your system develop the full human capacity for creativity and innovation? If so, not only will your workforce thrive and flourish, but your customers will stand in line waiting to do business with you.

HOW CAN I HELP?

For the remainder of my career, my mission is to help organizations capture the power of the 52 percent—those who are non-engaged because they have not been asked. To capture this missing voice will require designed leadership systems customized to each organization. I am not offering a one-size-fits-all solution. What I am offering is a structured approach to leadership that can be used as a framework for designing your unique system.

My approach to consulting has been developed for more than twenty-five years. I do not believe I have the best ideas. I do not believe I can walk into your organization and sell you an off-the-shelf system of leadership. From my research, each one is unique. That belief has shaped my career. I honestly believe the best ideas are already inside your organization. My job is to pull them out and organize them in a way that they can take root, grow, and flourish.

I invite you to call my personal cellphone number or email me to schedule a complimentary thirty- to sixty-minute session to see if we are a good fit.

(425) 269-8854
Dan@DanielEdds.com

BOOK DAN EDDS TO SPEAK AT YOUR NEXT EVENT

When it comes to choosing a professional speaker for your next event, you will find no one more thoughtful, respectful, and passionate about leadership than Dan Edds. Whether your audience is 5 or 5,000, in North America or abroad, Dan Edds will deliver a customized message of lasting and positive organizational change that will free the human spirit while creating the platform for elite organizational performance.

When you engage Dan's services, you will not get a retread of inspirational entertainment that will be forgotten by the end of the happy hour. Rather, Dan will deliver a thoughtful and comprehensive approach to leadership that will impact more than just your participants. Dan will be demonstrating an approach to organizational leadership that is being used by organizations that consistently operate at elite levels. His message will provide a transformational roadmap that will engage the entire workforce around transcendent values while driving award-winning performance.

Dan understands your audience does not want or need another lecture. They are already leaders or emerging leaders. However, Dan will challenge them through inspiring stories of organizational turnarounds and how exciting young leaders and organizations are innovating organizational leadership. The result is unparalleled organizational performance while the workforce flourishes.

To schedule a complimentary pre-speech phone interview, contact Dan at:

(425) 269-8854
Dan@DanielEdds.com

ABOUT THE AUTHOR

For twenty-five years, Daniel Edds has supported the public sector, healthcare, nonprofit, K-12 and higher-ed organizations as a management consultant. He holds a Master of Business Administration in International Business from the Alber's School of Business and Economics at Seattle University. He holds certifications in strategic planning and group facilitation. Dan is a Kaplan Norton Balanced Scorecard graduate and certified Lean practitioner. He has also held the Project Manager Professional certificate and is an experienced Baldrige Examiner through the Alliance program.

Leveraging the Genetics of Leadership: Cracking the Code of Sustainable Team Performance is Dan's second book. His first was *Transformation Management*, published by Spiro Press in 2003.

Dan lives in Bellevue, Washington not far from the world headquarters of Microsoft, T-Mobile, Expedia, and Amazon. His wife Kaye is a pediatric physical therapist for the local school district. Dan serves on the board of three nonprofits and finds time to volunteer at the Monroe Correctional Facility where he supports men in their personal journey of transformation. In his spare time, when it is available, he enjoys the challenge of capturing through photography the beauty and majesty of the outdoors. This might be a flower at the local botanical gardens, or one of the National Parks in the American Southwest. He continues to be a student of organizational transformation and how leadership can release the human capacity for innovation.